A Military Attaché in Japan

A Military Attaché in Japan

(1929–1933)

James G. McIlroy, Colonel, U.S. Army, Retired

VANTAGE PRESS
New York

Published by Vantage Press, Inc.
419 Park Ave. South, New York, NY 10016

Manufactured in the United States of America
ISBN: 978-0-533-15567-5

Library of Congress Catalog Card No.: 2006905973

0 9 8 7 6 5 4 3 2 1

Dedication
by Jane S. McIlroy
(author's daughter)

A heartfelt appreciation for an intelligent, honest, and conscientious father, who exhibited good diplomacy in his official contacts. As his daughter, I sense that I owe it to him to have this interesting historical account published.

Contents

Introduction
by Jane S. McIlroy
(author's daughter)

Who Is the Author?

An Ohio farm boy of Highland Scottish descent, third in a well-to-do family of three boys and two girls.

Personality?

Someone with a very wry sense of humor. A very moral man, who lived his life according to the West Point motto of "Duty-Honor-Country." He really had a soft heart, and his outlook definitely mellowed with his retirement from military life.

Credentials?

A West Point graduate, Class of 1904, graduating in the top fifth of his class, qualifying for an appointment in Engineering. He, however, desired to work with the foot soldier, hence chose the Infantry. From 1904–1908 he traveled extensively in Europe and Asia. One military assignment was to the Legation in China, where he had many memorable experiences. He mentioned attending a forty-course dinner at the Forbidden City, an invitation extended by the Dowager Empress to foreign officials. (Those who did not restrain their consumption during the early courses, were in bad shape at the end—for it was considered impolite to not eat some from each course!) From 1908–1912 he was one of the first selected for duty in Japan as a Language Student. While learning to speak, write, and read that difficult language, he also was to familiarize himself with the Japanese personality and the countryside, from a military perspective. During the U.S. participation in WWI, he was a Colonel in France on the Staff of General Pershing. Upon his return to the States, he was assigned to the Office of Far East Intelligence in Washington, D.C. In 1928 he received orders to again serve in Japan for a four-year tour as Military Attaché. During that time, he covered the start of WWII, as Japan invaded China.

Part 1
First Period, July 1929 to September 1931

I
The Appointment

First, what is a military attaché?

The War Department General Staff in Washington has a Military Intelligence Division. The duty of that division is expected to collect, evaluate, and distribute that information. When so treated it becomes Intelligence.

This information is secured from many sources. Naturally the best of this information should come from the expert living in each important foreign country. That expert is the Military Attaché. He is always an officer of our Army. He receives from the War Department an order to proceed to the capital of a certain foreign nation and there to report to the Chief of Mission at the American Embassy or Legation, that is to the Ambassador, Minister, or Chargé d'Affaires. He receives from the State Department a letter giving him temporary diplomatic status and attaching him to the particular Embassy or Legation. This letter gives him the diplomatic immunity that is intended to free him from the many petty annoyances the average citizen of this country may have to endure when in many other countries for business or pleasure.

So we may say that a Military Attaché is an Army officer resident in a foreign country with diplomatic status whose duty it is to secure information concerning that country as desired by the War Department.

In the fall of 1926 orders were sent to me from General Staff duty in Washington, D.C., to report for duty with troops at Fort Benjamin Harrison, near Indianapolis, Indiana. It was there in the early spring of 1929 while I was Executive of the 11th Infantry, the War Department wrote that they were considering me for the next military attaché to Tokyo, Japan, and asked if I would like to have that assignment. The decision was not an easy one to make as the Chief of Infantry had said that he would see that I went to the War College that year as a reward for my efficient handling of the 11th Infantry during a considerable period when no Colonel was in command. However, after a family conference, the reply sent back to Washington stated that I would be glad to go provided that a certain substantial addition could be made to my monthly salary, as I had a wife and five children and would want to take them all with me with the exception of my elder son.

The War Department surprised me by replying that the additional money was available and that they were satisfied as to my suitability for the position but, as no one in the office there knew my wife, would I please inform them as to her ability to handle her part as the wife of a Military Attaché.

A strange request it seemed to me. What would they expect a husband to say about his wife? But I had a happy thought. Walking over to my General's office the aide admitted me. To the General I said, "Good morning, General. I would like to show you a letter just received from the War Department." He took it, read it, smiled, and said, "I see your predicament. I suggest that you leave this letter with me. I think that I can handle this subject better than you."

About a week later word came back that I had been

designated as the next Military Attaché to Japan and that I must leave my post within two weeks, going by Army transport from Brooklyn, N.Y., after a two-week refresher course in Washington, D.C.

You can imagine the excitement that letter caused in our family. Naturally, there was a wild scramble to get our household goods packed and crated, buy what necessities in the way of clothing that we could, attend the many farewell dinners, and make the many good-bye calls.

One might naturally ask, why were you selected for this appointment? In my day when I knew something about how military personnel matters were handled in Washington, a Military Attaché was selected by the member of the Intelligence Division of the General Staff, who was known as the Liaison Officer. He kept in touch with the foreign Military Attachés in Washington and selected and kept in touch with our Military Attachés sent abroad. For the usual appointment of this sort the officers would look over the Army list and the officers' records to find one of proper rank, with good judgment, tact, social ability, and sufficient funds of his own outside his pay to properly handle the particular assignment. A few weeks of instruction in Washington prior to sailing had been deemed sufficient preparation for the job. At that time I had five children and little in the way of outside funds. Those two facts were enough to make me unsuitable for military attaché to the usual country.

But the policy in this respect had been slowly changing. In 1907, the War Department decided that as soon as possible their future Military Attachés to Japan and China would be officers who had been especially prepared for their duties. I believe that it was the celebrated General Leonard Wood to whom we must give credit for pushing the War Department to that decision. In 1908, four officers were selected and sent to Tokyo, Japan, and four to Peking, China. I was one of the four sent to Japan. To protect us from possible embarrassing situations we were attached to the legation. Our duty was to study the Japanese language. Later, in accord with my own efforts, the duties and studies of these student officers was much broadened. At the end of four years we were relieved by other officers. I believe that since 1908 there have always been student officers in that country until the outbreak of World War II. My selection as one of the first language students to Japan was probably influenced by the fact that I had already had one year of duty with the Legation Guard at Peking, China, and had traveled extensively in both the Far East and Europe. It is pleasing to believe also that my efficiency reports in the files of the War Department had something to do with my selection.

During those four years as a student in Japan I traveled much, not only in Japan, but throughout the Far East, and made the acquaintance of many Japanese and foreign businessmen and diplomatic persons of importance. During the First World War, I was on the staff of General Pershing at his headquarters. After the armistice, I was in Germany for some time. In 1923, orders sent me to Washington for duty in the Far Eastern Section of the Military Intelligence Division. There at first Major Short was my immediate chief. (Later Short was the General in command when the Pearl Harbor blow struck.) At first he had me in charge of Chinese Intelligence and completing and publishing the *Grammar of the Japanese Written Language*, which I had nearly finished in Japan when a student. Later he switched me to handle Japanese intelligence. Still later after Major Short had been sent to troops, I was placed in charge of the Section.

There as subordinates of mine were two Far Eastern experts; one, Major Karl Baldwin, who had been our Military Attaché to Japan during World War I, and who became the Military Attaché to Australia during World War II; the other, Major Robert Eichelberger, who in World War II became a Lieutenant General and commander of all American troops in Japan.

II
En Route to Japan

My orders required me to go by transport from Brooklyn. That meant a wonderful, long, interesting trip by way of the Panama Canal, San Francisco, Honolulu, the Philippines, and probably China. This was a grand prospect for my family but of little interest to me as I have never enjoyed life on the ocean deep. No doubt it will strike the reader as strange that we should be sent by such a time-consuming circuitous route. Naturally, it would seem more efficient for me to go alone to Washington for instructions, then return to my post, take my family and household goods with me to Seattle, and sail to Tokyo. This plan would have enabled us to delay our departure for two months. It would have made it possible for us all to be properly outfitted in clothing before departure, and it would have saved the wear and tear on our household goods.

It is thought that the controlling factor at that time was the financial side. Someone probably figured out that the transport route would be easier on the Army budget. Also, I recall that Congress was showing dangerous signs of wanting to do away with the entire transport system for the Army. So the Army needed all the personnel possible for each transport trip in order to show a low expense per head. It would have been too bad if Congress had done away with the Army transports, for we needed to have officers trained in such ocean transportation. No doubt those expert transportation officers were used to great advantage in World War II.

How we did it I do not know, but at the end of two weeks of packing, shopping, dining, and calling, we saw the Post Quartermaster truck away the last of our household goods and place them in a big boxcar billed to the Quartermaster base at Brooklyn, N.Y. Our last night at the post was spent as guests of the Commanding General and Mrs. Jamison in their lovely big quarters. A very thoughtful thing for them to do and certainly much appreciated by us. The next morning we all piled into our 1925 model Franklin Sedan and started on our interesting three-month trip. In the front seat with me was my second wife, Gwynneth, and my youngest daughter, Jane Susan, aged eight. In the rear seat were daughters, Margaret Edith, age sixteen, and Katharine Frances, age thirteen, and son, James Garfield, Jr., age fourteen. The elder son, Donald Scott had been left at the Y.M.C.A. in Indianapolis to go to college. (The mother of these children, Alberta Scott McIlroy, died unexpectedly at age thirty-four, when Jane Susan was three years old.)

Enroute to Washington we spent the first night at Irwin, Ohio, in the large old home where I was born, as guests of my brother and his wife, Mr. and Mrs. Glen G. McIlroy. The second night we were in a small hotel at Cambridge, Ohio. The following day, April 30, we reached Washington late in the afternoon. We went directly to the Highland Apartments on Connecticut Avenue. There lived my sister and her husband, Lieut. Colonel Walter S. Drysdale and their young son, Walter, Jr. They had arranged for us to occupy the attractive apartment adjacent to theirs. I recall still what a real thrill it gave us going

9

into those clean rooms. Our quarters at Fort Benjamin Harrison had been so dirty in comparison. The unsatisfactory condition there had been caused by our being compelled to use that very dirty impossible Indiana coal, not only in our furnace but in our kitchen range. The contrast was overwhelming and it put us in a very happy mood.

The next day Gwynneth went off for a two-day visit with her mother in Ottawa, Canada, while I reported to the officer in charge of Military Attachés in the Military Intelligence Division. He gave me an outline of the time to be spent by me in the various sections of the division during my two weeks in Washington.

My first visit was to the Geographic section located in the War College Building. There they showed me the maps of Japan already on file and told me about the work then going on in reproducing Japanese maps in a form that American officers could read. You see all real Japanese maps have the place names and data all written in the difficult Chinese ideographs. To translate those names and the data on the maps requires experts who know Japan and the Japanese language extremely well. There were not many such persons even in Japan. By knowing what maps we already had I would, when in Japan, be able to recognize a new map of value, if fortunate enough to see one.

In the Code Section (in another building) information was received about the various codes and ciphers available for use by Military Attachés and instruction given in their use. I was told of the danger of a foreign country being able to decipher our codes and about the way of going about getting a new code or cipher when it was thought that the ones in use had been broken by some country. They told me nothing about our own decoding section, not even its location, but I had known something about that when I had been on duty years before in the Far Eastern Section.

A visit to the Translation Section also was not necessary as I was familiar with it. When head of the Far Eastern Section I had often made use of it. It contained experts who could translate almost any language in the world. Some individuals employed there have been able to translate rapidly in eight different languages. For the knowledge they had I fear they were the poorest paid group in the United States.

In the information files of the Far Eastern Section most of the contents were already familiar to me, but I read important reports under various headings which had come in since my departure from that section.

Strange to say it was in the Finance Section where most of my time was spent. They told me the finance set up in the Tokyo office would be similar to that at a military post in the United States. Before World War I the financial affairs of a post were simple. The Post Quartermaster, whose primary duty was to handle supplies of the post, also kept the finance records. This detail he generally turned over to one or two sergeants in his office. These sergeants worked under his supervision and I never heard any serious growl from the Quartermaster about the difficulty of keeping those records. But during World War I, a special Finance Department was created. By the end of the war an office or organization of any size just had to have a Finance Officer with a lot of clerks to keep the complicated records, and to do the things financially in the way prescribed in the voluminous regulations which no combat officer had time to study and understand. So I well know that I was in for trouble in this line after arrival in Tokyo, for no matter how much I read or how much instruction I received in their office, it just was not going to stick and be available for use months later. Such a complicated procedure could only be learned by much experience. If permitted I will open up again on this subject about which I have some very strong feelings, when describing the work of Military Attaché in Tokyo.

During this busy time important calls were made on the chiefs of the Far Eastern Sections of the State, Navy, and Commerce Departments.

Gwynneth and I attended several interesting social affairs in the evening including a dinner by the Japanese Military Attaché and one by my sister. At the latter I found myself sitting beside the attractive wife of the then Japanese Naval Attaché. We had been friends during my student days in Japan at which time she was the attractive young daughter of the brilliant Admiral Miobara. Later in Japan, she and Gwynneth became very friendly.

Naturally Gwynneth did more shopping for herself and the children. At our last post, we had permitted our clothing supply to run down because we did not want to invest in new articles until we knew where our next station would be. For instance, Alaska and Panama require quite different clothing.

We learned that a new ruling made it impossible for us to take the automobile on the transport with us. So we had to sell in a hurry. The unpleasant result was that our $3,200 Franklin Sedan, model 1925 went for $400. And we all knew that a car would be necessary in Tokyo. Certainly fortune did not shine on us in that situation.

Before leaving Washington I went in to make my farewell call on the General in charge of the Military Intelligence Division. It was then and there I received my principal mission while in Japan. It was to make a thorough study of and report on how best to bomb Japan from the air. That was to be my number one secret duty during the first two years of my tour as Military Attaché to Japan.

We were required to report at the Army Transport Base in Brooklyn three days before the scheduled date of sailing, so after two busy weeks in the Capital we took the train for New York. From Pennsylvania Station we went to the base in Brooklyn by subway, a new experience for the children. Later an Army truck was sent over for our personal baggage. At the base we were glad to find small but comfortable rooms available for us all on the Hostess Floor.

At this time we were carefully checked to see that we had received all the injections and had been vaccinated as required by transport regulations. If anything was lacking in our records they gave it to us right there. Again we did some shopping for the family, as we knew we should be well outfitted by the time we reached Tokyo so that we would make a proper appearance from the start. However, I did take the time to go with my eldest daughter, Margaret, by a long subway ride and ferry trip to Governor's Island to show her the Army quarters (house) at Fort Jay where she was born in 1913.

It was good news, at this time, to learn that our household goods had arrived and had been placed on the transport. It was more than good news—it was a great relief. A soldier, from long training, is most uneasy when separated from his supplies and equipment.

At last we were aboard the transport and soon moved out on our long trip to San Francisco. At our right rear was Governor's Island where I had been stationed as a Lieutenant of the 29th Infantry in 1912 and 1913. On our right we passed the Statue of Liberty and later went out the strait between the two old forts, Wadsworth on Staten

Island on the right and Hancock on Long Island on our left.

The city of Colon at the Atlantic end of the Panama Canal was to be our first stop. Enroute we passed the Bahamas, and sailed between Cuba and Haiti. Rapidly it became warmer and warmer. Having been stationed for years in the north I was not equipped with late style summer uniform. In fact I had thrown away what light weight uniforms I had before leaving my last post because I realized that I must show up in the latest and best only. Fortunately the commanding officer of the transport permitted the officers who were not on duty with the troops aboard to wear civilian clothes.

As we sailed southward through the islands of the West Indies, there happened nothing of special interest to recall. I read what books I could find in the library about those islands but generally speaking there was an awful shortage of instructive and informative books in the transport library. Ninety-nine percent of the books were cheap novels.

We arrived off the western end, yes, I said western, of the canal in the early morning. After breakfast we all went ashore. First on our list of things to do was shopping at the big canal commissary in Colon. Among other things we bought there was a complete set of beautiful English Minton china for twelve. It was so much cheaper there than in the United States as there was no duty included in the price, in fact the price was wholesale with a small addition for overhead. However, those barrels of china were an additional responsibility that we had to watch carefully all the way to Tokyo.

In Colon I also invested in some Marine Corps shirts and trousers to wear on the transport during the hotter parts of our transport trip.

In the Commissary we made the acquaintance of an Army Chaplain stationed in the Canal Zone. He kindly offered to take us in his motor car and show us the Atlantic end of the Zone. Did we appreciate his kindness? He took us to the Gatun Locks, and drove us about the country. The family saw their first banana trees with fruit on them. We called on the Commanding Officer at Fort Randolph, who was a classmate of mine at West Point. He insisted on our coming back there for an early dinner.

I still remember the ride we had that evening in a funny old carriage, drawn by a funny little horse, and driven by a funny Negro driver, through the funny streets of that funny city of Colon. That city impressed me as being the type that one should expect as the result of being the playground of sailors from all nations. Our family went into one of the open front cafés for liquid refreshments but from what we saw we were glad to get outside and decided we would not risk another such adventure.

That night we passed through the canal. We stayed up to see our transport pass through the Gatun Locks and be impressed by the quiet, simple, efficient manner by which our boat was moved along by all concerned. Then we went to bed.

During our stay in the Panama Canal area we heard much to cause us to think that the canal was extremely vulnerable, but after passing through World War II we must conclude either that it was not so vulnerable or else that our military personnel did a superb job of protecting it. It pleases me to believe the latter.

When we again looked out our portholes we were well out in the Bay of Panama, well on our way to San Francisco. No stop had been made at the Pacific end of the canal.

Going up the west coast of Central America and Mexico there was little of interest. It was a quiet, lazy voyage, very hot with no breeze. The sea was glassy, spotted here and there with large turtles, sleeping, with usually a bird sitting on the back of each. Often those turtles would not awaken until we had almost struck them with our prow. Then they would dive and swim rapidly away, while the bird circled above awaiting its reappearance. In this part of the ocean the children saw their first flying fish. Our youngest child saw her first porpoises at their play but they were not new to the other children, who had often seen them when we spent three months on the shore near Panama City in Florida.

From Brooklyn to San Francisco the senior officer on board was Major General LeJeune, Commandant of the Marine Corps. The only other time I had ever seen the general was in Belgium after the armistice in the fall of 1918. One evening I arrived at the city hall of Arlon in the southeastern corner of that country. My duty was that of a special observer for General Pershing. The American Second Division was spending the night in that area. General LeJeune was in command. The Division Head-quarters were at the city hall. I dismissed my chauffeur and interpreter and proceeded to sit the evening out with the division staff, as they supervised the forward move-ment of the subordinate units and their own headquar-ters group. By midnight they were all gone and to my surprise I found myself to be the only human being left in that big Hotel de Ville. Looking for a place to sleep I found a huge State bedroom on the second floor rear. Here I had a good rest and in the morning found the place still unoc-cupied. Dressing quickly I went to the rest room, which I found in a disgraceful condition. Walking out into the gar-den in the rear, the view that met my eyes was certainly not to the credit of American troops.

I knew that the Rainbow Division was due in that area by noon that day and I could picture the disgust of their commander, General MacArthur, when he arrived at Arlon and found the unsanitary situation left by the headquarters of the Second Division. So after my men had brought me some breakfast we moved forward to visit other troops but on the way I passed through General LeJeune's new command post. I stopped and went in to see him. He and his Chief of Staff were terribly chagrined when they heard my story about how they had left their former command post for General MacArthur. They begged me not to report the matter to General Pershing and promised to send a truck load of men back at once to clean up the situation. During our several talks on the transport neither of us ever mentioned the above incident.

There as another subject of considerable interest about which we did talk at great length. We were laughing about the Army's very faulty uniform for the summer. For years the Army had used an American-made cloth that changed color every time it was washed so that soon in any company each soldier had his own individual colored uniform. The exception to this situation was in the Philippines where the troops managed to secure the British-made high grade fast colored "Hong Kong khaki." My indignant questions to him were: Why did our Army use the American cloth when it could buy the superior fast color cloth from the British? Why could his Marines have that high grade fast color cloth when the Army still had to use that old inferior grade? His reply was very enlightening to me. His reply was to this effect: "Good fast colored cotton cloth for uniforms could have been made in the United States long ago. When I became Commandant of the Marine Corps I insisted on having a better uniform for my corps. There was quite a fight but I stood fast, determined not to buy until I could secure good cloth. Finally the cloth firms did come across with the material which is now used by the Marines." A few years later the Army adopted that same cloth. General LeJeune was evidently quite proud of his having been able to secure that excellent cotton cloth for the Marines. This conversation started from the General having noted with some amusement that I, an Army officer, was wearing a pair of new Marine trousers.

Seventeen days after leaving Brooklyn we passed through the Golden Gate and docked at Fort Mason. This was a quartermaster's depot used especially for handling transports to and from the Panama Canal and Honolulu. This was the end of the run for that transport, so everyone disembarked bag and baggage.

By a study of a map and doing a little figuring I estimated that our family had now traveled 5,758 miles since leaving our post at Fort Benjamin Harrison, Indiana. The distance from that post to San Francisco by rail is about 2,340 miles. In other words, the sea route had been about 3,418 miles farther. In time our trip had consumed, not counting our stop in Washington, twenty-three days. Had we come by train it would have required three days. These figures are given with reference to my remarks along this line on page 55.

At Fort Mason we took quarters in the Hostess House on the Fort. We could get our meals at a cafeteria on the post but often went out to enjoy one of the many interesting restaurants of the city. Fort Mason is really surrounded by the city so one could walk to good restaurants or go downtown by tram in twenty minutes.

One of Gwynneth's sisters and her husband motored

up from San Francisco to help us enjoy the city for a few days.

As soon as my household goods were placed on the dock I made a careful inspection of the boxes and crates. Many of them were found in a weakened condition. With a hammer I did such repairing and strengthening as seemed to be demanded.

Of course during the ten days we were in San Francisco, Gwynneth took the opportunity to do a lot of shopping. Gradually our clothing requirements were being filled.

At the end of those pleasant ten days in San Francisco we were loaded aboard another transport which then sailed for Honolulu and other points west.

This was the third time I had sailed for the Orient, the first time for the family. Shortly after passing through the Golden Gate the transport began a very perceptible roll. From my own experience and from what my friends have told me I believe that it is always rough outside the Gate. Although the roughness did not bother the family, it did me. My feelings have always gone up and down in contradiction to the waves, so that I have never looked forward with pleasure to a sea voyage. If you will pardon a few reminiscences here—there comes to me very clearly the experience of my sister and me when going from Manila to Hong Kong in a small liner in 1904. A typhoon struck us soon after departure from Manila and lasted until we arrived at Hong Kong. During those three days we did not see each other, as each stuck close to his bunk—that is as close as the pitching and rolling of the boat permitted. But how quickly we recovered after anchor had been cast at Hong Kong, and I have never forgotten that first wonderful meal we had in a good hotel ashore. But the biggest waves I have ever seen were off the Aleutian Islands in the fall of 1911. They were truly mountain high. At that time I tried to test the theory thoroughly that if a person will only stay right up on deck and take it he will in time become accustomed to the situation and lose his sea sickness. Well, it did not work with me. So after a horrible experience lasting all day I gave up and weakly found my way to my bunk where I remained until we had almost reached Seattle.

On this new transport we were pleased to find a Lieutenant Thomas G. Cranford, the newly appointed Assistant Military Attaché to Tokyo. He also was a former language student in Japan. We were destined to work very closely together for the next several years.

On this trip from San Francisco my rank was sufficient to secure for us cabins up on the Promenade deck. This was quite a contrast to the accommodations I received when a young lieutenant fresh from the Academy. Then I was bunked in the hospital part of the ship, way down near the rudder in the lower of a two-tier bunk, with about twenty more of my classmates, all going to the Philippines. Almost every minute of the day and night the noisy machinery went on to turn the rudder every so little, and as we neared the Philippines the heat down in that poorly ventilated hole was almost unendurable.

In the adjoining cabins on our deck was a very interesting family from the Navy, Commander and Mrs. Bradley and their four tall attractive daughters, going to the island of Guam where he was to become the Governor.

From San Francisco we had a new senior officer aboard. It was Major General Paul S. Malone who was going to the Philippines to take command of the Infantry Division with headquarters at Fort McKinley near Manila. He was just chock-full of energy and expected everyone else to be. At once, he began to arrange for all sorts of entertainment. A string band was organized from the Filipino personnel aboard. There were movies, boxing bouts, dances, lectures on various islands as we approached them, etc. All such matters received his personal aggressive attention. To please him, everyone had to be busy doing something. Probably it was good for us. He required us to show up for dinner each evening in our best uniform or in a tuxedo. I chose the latter as I had not yet been able to have made any suitable summer uniforms.

Honolulu, of course, was our first stop. It was a most pleasing arrival. On the dock was the Army band doing its best to make everyone happy. There was quite a crowd of service people and civilians, their arms full of leis, their hands waving, waiting to welcome their expected friends. As we approached the dock slowly there were many dark-skinned natives diving very deep for the coins thrown from the deck by the passengers. We knew of no friends of ours in the city, so imagine our surprise when a distinguished appearing gentleman and two lovely young ladies came up to us while we were still on deck and after weighing us down with leis explained that the girls were cousins of mine from near my old home in Ohio, and that their gentleman friend was the Acting Governor of the Hawaiian Islands, all three at our service for the day. I learned later that the young ladies were teachers at the Episcopal school in the city. It was also of much interest to me to learn that that school was largely supported by gifts from William C. Proctor of the well-known soap firm of Proctor and Gamble of Cincinnati, Ohio. I had had the good fortune to know Mr. Proctor quite well but to the best of my memory he had never mentioned to me any charities that he had established.

Twice before I had visited Honolulu but this promised to be the best of my visits there, and it turned out that way. Soon, we were placed in a motor car and then began a tour deluxe. We went everywhere and apparently saw everything and did everything that was to be done. We visited the pineapple fields and there ate a ripe pineapple. Its taste was so superior to those we get in the United States, no comparison. We lunched at the country club. We had tea at the Royal Hawaiian. In all, it was a most delightful day with three such ideal entertainers. But all good things must have an end. That evening, the band and many friends with leis saw the transport pull away from the dock for Guam, our next stop.

I have visited Honolulu four times in my life. It has always been a pleasant experience. The officials and residents were so hospitable to visitors. And the setting was so romantic and enjoyable. It is hoped that the great construction projects of World War II have not spoiled its attractive features.

In those days, one of the big problems for intelligence personnel of the Army and Navy was to find out and predict correctly what action the Japanese people of those islands would take in case of a war with Japan. It is believed that we were all surprised at what did happen when the real test came. I understand that almost 100 percent were found loyal to the United States.

From Honolulu to Guam we continued the strenuous life under the guidance of General Malone even though the temperature became warmer and warmer.

We passed within sight of Wake Island but all we could see was a low lying strip of ground with a small shack thereon, probably a radio or cable station.

One matter of interest to us all was the romance that developed rapidly between the eldest daughter of the Naval officer next cabin to us and a handsome young Army officer just out of West Point. He was to be stationed in the Philippines. Everyone wondered whether she would be willing to get off the transport and remain at Guam with her family or would insist on going on to the Philippines on that same transport to be married.

On our way to Guam the family had to listen to the story of my visit there twenty-five years before. How I had taken the belle of the boat ashore in a row boat; how it had rained hard while we were still in the boat, running the blue out of the gorgeous big hat down over her white shirtwaist; how we had ridden on a bull cart the several miles to the island's capital where in spite of the blue-streaked shirtwaist we had attended the tea given by the then Naval Governor; how the Governor and his wife had been unable to keep his three grown daughters helping to entertain the guests because they had got hold of the mail brought by the transport. Then the question naturally arose—Can it be that a group of daughters was a prerequisite for the position of Governor of that island? Or was it rather the case where Naval officers with daughters sought that particular assignment? I can't blame them if true, for there were many attractive Army, Navy, and Marine officers to be met with on that island and in cruising about in the Naval Supply boat to the Philippines, Japan, and China.

Well, upon arrival off the port of Guam we went ashore to see our Naval friend made Governor. As I recall, the older three children accompanied us. The youngest, Jane Susan lost out and had to remain on board because the General had issued instructions that children under ten would not go ashore. (She was nine plus years.)

Our visit to the island was most interesting. We had been looking forward to this visit and certainly it turned out to be more enjoyable than had been expected. This time a small motor boat took us from the transport to the small wharf. We passed over the coral reefs, which we could see near the surface in the clear sea water. They looked very dangerous to small boats—their jagged points. But they were beautiful in their variegated coloring.

As we approached the shore, the guns boomed a welcome to the new Governor. The island government had declared a holiday. On shore, we saw the Navy family placed in the island's best motor car for their triumphal trip to the capital several miles distant. The native school children all in white had been placed along the road with their arms full of flowers, which they scattered in front of the new Governor's car as it approached. So, in a way, he truly rode to the office on a bed of flowers.

The natives were pleasing in appearance. They are known as Chemorros. In them is Polynesian, Spanish, and probably a little of several other types of blood. Under American administration since the Spanish-American War they had made great strides in education and in their living conditions.

We managed to get in another car and followed the Navy family along the beautiful shore drive to the capital, Agana.

The inauguration ceremony was held in a grove near the Governor's House, the same one used by the Spanish Governor before we took over in—was it 1898? Our family sat in the front row of seats at the ceremony as important witnesses of the event.

The island of Guam at that time was a beautiful romantic tropical place but from what I have read the necessities of World War II left little of its beauty.

As we weighed anchor for Manila there was that young Army officer but his companion was missing. She had remained in Guam with her family. I suspect that her mother had much to do with that decision.

After leaving Guam, there was just a strenuous hot time had by all. No land was in sight until we reached the Philippines and started through the narrow passage between the most southern point of the large island of Luzon and the most northern tip of the island of Samar. It is a marvelous sail through San Bernardino Strait into the South China Sea and then by the great fortress of Corregidor into Manila Bay.

Upon arrival at the wharf of Manila, most of the officers and their families left us to go to their various stations in the islands where they would remain for at least the next two years. Our two older daughters were taken by their cousin, Dorothy Hossie Taylor, to visit her and her husband in their Army quarters on the island of Corregidor. Our boy and youngest girl were taken by the parents of friends of theirs who had lived near us at Fort Benjamin Harrison—taken out to their quarters at Fort McKinley. Gwynneth and I decided that it would be cooler, cheaper, and more convenient for us to remain right on the transport in our excellent cabins.

Soon all the freight had been unloaded on the dock and placed in a large warehouse thereon. Before long nearly all of it had been removed except our household goods. Then it was that I again spent time in repairing crates that had been broken or had become loose.

Our first trip was made to Fort McKinley to call on the officer and his family who had so kindly taken over our two young children. They drove us about the country in the vicinity of Manila. I again realized how much it is much like Japan. It is no wonder that the Japanese have always coveted those islands, and that they have migrated there whenever it has been possible to work their way in. Life for them requires little adjustment in the Philippines.

Near the end of our stay at Manila we took the two children from Fort McKinley by Army boat out to Corregidor to spend the night with their cousins. Dorothy had a decided house full, six of us, but handled it very nicely. Her husband was the then Major Victor V. Taylor, Adjutant General of the island. Their quarters were large and had a fine location overlooking the entrance to Manila Bay with its two small fortified islands.

In the late afternoon they had a cocktail party for Gwynneth and me. The cocktails were the weakest I had ever tasted but they were good and so we were able to drink many of them before we obtained the effect that one would probably produce in a colder climate. It probably is a good custom to follow in a hot climate where plenty of H_2O is needed.

On the military side, I took time necessary to talk with the Intelligence group at the military headquarters in Manila and to read much of interest in their files. Of especial interest to me were their war plans for defense of the Philippines and various accounts of intelligence agents who had been watching the activities of the Japanese not only in the Philippines but in other parts of the Far East. When at Corregidor, Major Taylor, as guide showed me much of its secret defenses.

One day we had a delightful luncheon at the quarters of Colonel and Mrs. Otis Horney. The reason back of this invitation was that Col. Horney was appointed to West Point from the same section of Ohio as I was. Even when a young boy, people were always telling me fine things about that Horney boy who had gone to West Point. Well, Horney was in the Ordnance Department. It is well known in the Army that officers of the Ordnance always have well-constructed and well-cared-for quarters. This was no exception. It was a quaint old Spanish home of much dignity and comfort located right on top of the old wall of the city of Manila. Our dessert that day is remembered because it was unusual—an ice cream made from the milk of the coconut. We were told that the daughter was then working on a plan to can that product for sale all over the world. I wonder what became of that seemingly good idea for I have never seen anything of the sort on a groceryman's shelves.

In between times Gwynneth shopped for dresses and luncheon sets while I strove to have a couple of uniforms made.

The middle of the days were very hot. I quite approve of their custom of taking an afternoon siesta. This custom is apparently followed there by everyone who can possibly get away with it. The Army had the sensible policy of starting to work very early in the morning and then stopping for the day about noon.

After ten days at Manila the transport was again well loaded with freight and the officers and their families returning to the United States after their tour in the islands. As the transport was about to sail, General MacArthur came aboard to say good-bye to friends. He looked his usual handsome, friendly, distinguished self. At that time he was in command of all our military forces in the Philippines.

Our next stop was to be Chinwangtao in northern China. As we ploughed north we passed along the very rough and forbidding eastern shore of the island of Formosa, on into the East China Sea, through the muddy waters caused by the large Yangtze River, on into and through the Yellow Sea, with its muddy waters from the great Hoang Ho River on into the Gulf of Peichili.

On the way up, there was little of interest. The passengers were nearly all strangers to us. A Coast Artillery Colonel was in command. He quickly announced the white dress uniform for dinners. I had to wear my new white mess jacket with black trousers which I had with much trouble managed to have made in Manila. This made me conspicuous at dinners but there was no help for it. It had been impossible for me to secure any other uniforms at Manila because all the tailors were rushed with orders from all the newly arrived officers off our transport. They all wanted summer uniforms as quickly as they could be obtained.

As we went north near Formosa I had the unusual privilege of seeing an immense sea mammal or fish. It appeared alongside the transport when I was the only person observing from that side of the boat. It was black and gray in color, about twenty feet long, and quite large around its center. It dived directly under our transport. No one aboard, including the Captain, could tell me what it was from my description. It looked to me like a cross between a whale and a shark.

As we weighed anchor, a young officer of our Engineer Corps, a Lieutenant Twitty, reported to me stating that he had been ordered to Tokyo as a language student.

The purpose of the side trip to Chinwangtao was to disembark the officers, their families, troops, and baggage going to Tientsin and Peking for station. Practically all other officers and their families, as soon as we docked, left the transport and hurried to the station to take the first train north at the sea end of the Great Wall of China. Arriving at our destination we went out into the street adjoining the station to secure transportation to the Great Wall. For transportation there was nothing but rikashas. The street was full of them. What a noisy time that was with the rikasha men yelling to each other and to the passengers and friends among the passengers yelling back and forth to each other as they selected their vehicle and runners. This was all an old story for me as I had lived in China one year and in Japan four years when I was a young lieutenant. But it was a new experience for Gwynneth and I suspect for all that large party except me.

Here Gwynneth had a mishap, which in all my years in the Orient, I never saw before or since. It was quite evident to me as she slowly took her place in the rikasha in front of me that she was none too sure that she was doing the sensible thing. And her evident misgivings were soon confirmed. Hardly was she seated when her coolie let the shafts go slowly upward and backward finally turning her over backward into the muddy street. Going quickly to her rescue, we found there was no damage done except to her dignity. Why that coolie did that will never be known. He himself appeared surprised. Perhaps he was drunk or under the influence of opium. Bravely Gwynneth took another rikasha but I fear she did not enjoy the ride.

Anyway we went through the dirty muddy streets between the one-story mud-walled huts from which the natives came forth hastily to have a look see at the crazy barbarians in their midst.

The wall was a sight to well repay us all for the trouble of the trip. However, I would say that it is not as impressive at the sea end as it is well to the interior. I saw it first in 1904 at a place northwest of Peking. As I stood there on top of it and looked at it winding up and down along the ridges and over the highest peaks of the mountains far into the distance it gave me quite a thrill. It brought to my mind a well-remembered sentence in our country school geography about the "mythical wall of China." It was a tremendous undertaking for those days—two thousand miles of it. For centuries, it served its purpose, to help protect China from her enemies to the north. Now, it is only an ancient relic, though still in fairly good condition. Seeing that great wall one can begin to understand how our air force during the recent war found it possible to get that big super bomber base constructed in western China by coolie labor.

Near our dock at Chinwangtao was a liner being coaled up. Those many Chinese coolies, like a nest of ants carrying the coal in small baskets into the bunkers of the ship, were the dirtiest human beings I have ever seen. This sight of so much cheap labor was an unusual experience for Americans.

Being at Chinwangtao reminded me of my visit there in 1905 shortly after the end of the Japanese-Russian War. I was sent up there from Peking to receive from an expected American transport ninety soldier re-enforcements from the Philippines for the Legation Guard in Peking.

During my stay there I was living at a very small hotel. There I found a Frenchman, a German, and an Irishman who had passed through the United States and so claimed to be American and several other nationalities. We sat at one large table. Every meal, there were loud heated arguments over world history. When the situation grew too tense the Irishman would throw in some funny remark that would save the day.

Looking around for a means of unloading the transport when it did arrive, I found that nearly everything in that port was owned or at least controlled by the British. After much difficulty and persistence, I managed to get into the inner sanctum to see the head Britisher. He seemed displeased by my call. I tried my best to make some plan with him for unloading those soldiers and their baggage and getting them out of that place as soon as possible. All he would say was, "Oh, see me again after the transport comes in and we will see what can be done."

The British had some sort of a club there but I was not invited into it.

It was a lonely vigil I had there for about ten days. Twice a day I took a long walk out to the end of a small point of land to search the sea for a sight of that American transport. It seemed to me it would never come.

By arrangement with an official of the Chinese railway there were set aside for use of the men and their baggage two coaches and a baggage car. Some Russian officer offered me the use of a Russian barracks nearby, but I had orders not to be friendly with the Russians at that time. No, I think my orders were more nearly this—not to accept favors from them. Our people at that time were very pro-Japanese.

One day from the point a beautiful picture awaited me—the sun shining on a large white boat coming slowly in with the American flag flying at her stern. All this time, I had been in uniform with side arms—a good long Smith and Wesson. Immediately I hurried to see the head Britisher. He was not at his office. Feeling desperate I went right down to the wharves. There there were quite a number of boats of various kinds and sizes, most of them controlled by the British. Picking out the largest, I went aboard and up to the bridge where the Chinese captain was found. I said to him, "You are to take me out to that American transport and bring ashore some American troops." He seemed not to hesitate. He probably thought I had authority from the British office.

About the time the transport had anchored out in the

bay we were alongside. Running up on deck, I was received with much interest by the officers and their families aboard on their way back from the Philippines to the United States.

Soon the Filipino crew was loading the baggage of the ninety soldiers aboard my boat. Not much would go below deck so most of it had to be piled on deck, and when the baggage was aboard those ninety six-footers also came down onto the deck of that little boat. Both the Chinese captain and I were now alarmed that our boat was top heavy. Believe me it was a relief when we tied up at the wharf. The soldiers unloaded their own baggage and placed it in the baggage car and then took seats in the day coaches.

And then came the rub. Although I tried very hard there proved to be no way for me to get those cars rolling for Peking that night. I suspected that the Britisher was making me pay for my unauthorized action in taking out that boat of his. So the men had to sit up all night in those uncomfortable wooden seats. But we did get under way the next morning and arrived safely in Peking that afternoon. To this day I do not know whether the British were ever paid for the use of their boat and I don't care. In those days they were hard to deal with. At that time, the Germans were outdoing them in the Far East. The German would go out of his way to get business and he was more pleasant to deal with. I often predicted in those days that if the British did not soon go to war against the Germans they would find most of their commerce in the Far East taken away from them. This is a good place to sound a warning to American businessmen abroad—to not let themselves drift into that cock-of-the-walk attitude that was so common among the British in the days of their world supremacy.

III
Arrival in Japan

At last we were headed directly for Japan. As we moved into the harbor of Nagasaki in the early morning it was a beautiful picture we saw through our portholes. Soon we were all on deck to enjoy the scenery with its many green terraced hills all about the harbor. We did not waste much time at breakfast. Our diplomatic passport enabled us to go through the Japanese customs with no trouble and soon we found ourselves, bag and baggage, in rooms at the Hotel du Japan, which was located on the side of a hill not far from the bay.

While we were sitting there in our room Gwynneth remarked that she was thirsty and would like a glass of water. I called a "boy" and told him "O mizu ippai kudasai" (Honorable cold water one glass please). He replied with a quick short "Hai" (yes), bowed and went out. Then suddenly realizing that I also was thirsty I clapped my hands again. When the boy returned I added "Nihai, dozo" (two glasses please). Now when we lived at Fort Benjamin Harrison near Indianapolis everywhere we drove in our car we saw big advertisements on roadside billboards about the soft drink called Nehi (pronounced knee high). The big pictures showed a beautiful girl seated with pretty legs to her knees at least, and alongside a bottle of Nehi standing and reaching to her knees;

with a statement in large letters, "Keep your eye on the bottle." So when Gwynneth heard me say "nihai" (same pronunciation as the Nehi) she looked over at me curiously and said, "Are you trying to be cute? You know they would not have any Nehi here." And that brought an explosion from me. Well, anyhow Nihai was the first word of Japanese the family learned.

I recall the incident when I learned my first Japanese word. It was back in 1905. An American friend and I had gone ashore in that very Nagasaki. Approaching a storekeeper on the street to our surprise he said "Ohio." To my friend, I said, "How do you suppose he knew I was from Ohio?" But when the next storekeeper bowed and said the same word, we knew it was a greeting of some kind and upon inquiry learned it was "Good Morning." That was my first word of Japanese. Little did I know then that I was to spend the greater part of four years trying to learn that impossible language.

While in Nagasaki, in fact before we left the transport, I had a talk with the American Army Quartermaster concerning our household goods aboard. He assured us that he would do his best to expedite its shipment on to Tokyo. You see the U.S. Quartermaster Department detailed for two-year tours to Nagasaki one of their officers to look after our Army's supply matters in that city. His main duty was to look after arrangements for coaling our transports when they called there, usually about once a month. The job was known to be about the easiest in the Army.

That first day ashore I visited the Nagasaki Branch of the Hong Kong-Shanghai Bank and cashed a U.S. Treasury check for about 100 dollars, receiving in exchange about 225 yen in bills. At the bank window I put the bills all in my wallet and then the wallet in my left hip pocket. But just before leaving the bank I happened to recall my elder brother's caution to me once that the right front trouser watch pocket was the best place to store away a roll of bills as it is the most difficult pocket for a pickpocket to operate in without your being aware of it. So I then and there shifted my wad of big Japanese bills, a wise move as you will soon see.

At 2:00 P.M. the day following our arrival in Japan we entrained for Tokyo. Our first stop was at Moji at the western entrance to the Inland Sea. Here we had to detrain and take a large ferry boat to Shimonoseki, which is just opposite Moji across the strait. As we crossed the strait we sat on the upper deck. Lt. Twitty was with us. When the ferry docked we moved down the wide stairway toward the gangplank as a part of a big crowd of passengers. We were the only foreigners. I had a package in my left arm and was holding Gwynneth's left arm with my right hand. There was some pushing by the crowd. At one time I noticed a Japanese girl very close between Gwynneth and me as though she were trying to push through between us. At that time I called to Lieutenant Twitty who was below us on the stairs, "Look out Twitty. This is a good place for pickpockets." As soon as we crossed the gangplank I stepped to one side and felt for my money. The wallet was gone, but the roll of bills was still in my watch pocket. Twitty told me that he had noticed a boy and girl rush off the boat ahead of all others. In my wallet was a U.S. Treasury check for one month's salary and twenty-five dollars. I reported the theft to the police but without any favorable results. It was not so bad for in the end I was out but twenty-five dollars. The government check in time was duplicated. This was our first experience in a Japanese crowd.

That evening we took a first class train from

Shimonoseki for Tokyo. We had a comfortable night in our berths. The next day there was so much of interest. It was a pleasure for me to see the family enjoying that trip. Everything was so new to them. It was like being in a fairyland or a never-never land. But after awhile the children tired of looking at the scenery. However, Gwynneth kept up her interest in everything she saw, asking me no end of questions. My four years as a student in Japan made me a walking encyclopedia for the family in things Japanese. Made me feel a little important for a change.

From our windows, there was no end to the beautiful scenery and interesting objects to observe; on our left the mountains, the waterfalls, the rice paddies, and the little village with their bright colored tile roofs nesting in the valleys. On our right, the Inland Sea with its distant islands, its shipping, the little bays one after another, lined with the old gnarled pines so twisted by the winds, the fishermen, and the many clam diggers.

I am not a socialist but one must admit that government ownership of the railways seemed to work well in Japan. The officials and employees all wore a black uniform, always most neat and clean. Station masters and higher officials wore a short sword at their side. All employees appeared to be very much on the job and proud of that job. However, their railways did appear to require about twice the personnel of our privately run railway companies. The trains ran on time. The cars were kept clean. There were three classes of cars for passengers. A wide painted band just below the windows and extending around the car announced its particular class, red for third class, blue for second, and white for first. The working class and students were usually found in third class; well-to-do Japanese and resident foreigners in second;

and Japanese officials, diplomats, and tourists in first class.

At the station your ticket is inspected and punched as you pass through a narrow gate to your train. No one looks at it while you are on the train but it is taken up at the exit gate as you leave your train at your destination.

The dinners on the express trains were passable but nothing to brag about. Their coffee, especially, I never could enjoy. However, at many stations one could buy through your window a neat appetizing foreign or Japanese style luncheon put up in a clean pine box. At almost any station one could purchase for two cents a little earthen pot of tea and a small cup. At a few, if he knew the ropes, one could secure a quart bottle of cold beer.

The Japanese railroad tracks are narrow gauge. The seats in most cars extend along the sides facing each other. You must look out for your feet that they are not stepped on by people passing by in the aisle.

A Japanese who is asleep just stretches out on one of those long seats and is soon lost to the world. Even were a car to become crowded with passengers standing, a Japanese lying down would not think of sitting up to make it possible for others to sit down, and strange to say those standing up never seem to expect any consideration from those already on a seat. It was a common sight in Japan in warm weather to see a Japanese dressed in foreign style clothing when he came aboard the train stand on the seat in the presence of women, remove all his clothing except his loin cloth, and put on a light colored cotton kimono so that he would be more comfortable for the trip. Before reaching his destination he would reverse the operation so that he could step off the train and meet his friends and relatives all dressed up in his foreign clothes.

Our train passed through many tunnels and deep

cuts. We must admit that the Japanese construction engineers were amazingly efficient in the construction of the stone work at the entrances to those tunnels and in the retaining walls built on the mountain side of the cuts.

Now and then we saw a hydro-electric power plant, the position of which I took notice of for future use in reporting bombing objectives. And, of course, I was much interested in the great steel works at Yawata in Kyushu, on the north side of the railway, shortly before we arrived at Moji. I knew there were great industrial plants along the Inland Sea but the railway had a way of skirting around some hill which would obscure just such things of interest to a Military Attaché.

Twenty-eight hours after leaving Shimonoseki we arrived at 9:00 P.M. at the Tokyo main station, known as Shimbashi station. Walking from the train along the concrete platform we were most conscious of the loud clatter of the wooden "geta" (shoes) worn by most of the Japanese passengers, especially by those in the third class cars. That night we spent in the Station Hotel, which was on the second floor of the station building itself. We were quite comfortable in that foreign type hotel and very glad to have our long journey of ninety days and 18,000 miles at an end.

IV

Karuizawa

The morning after our arrival in Tokyo, Colonel and Mrs. Burnett called on us. He had been the Military Attaché for the past four years and was now to turn over to me and return by the next transport to the United States. Colonel Burnett at that time was the only officer of our Army who knew as much or more about the Japanese than I did. He, like I, had been a language student in Japan for four years. While I was in the Far Eastern Section of the Military Intelligence Division of the General Staff in Washington, he was serving a four-year term as the Military Attaché in Tokyo. It was during that period, September 1923, that occurred the Great Earthquake which killed so many tens of thousands and almost destroyed both Yokohama and Tokyo. It was Burnett from whom I received the information daily that enabled me to keep the Secretary of War, Mr. Weeks, and our President personally informed about the situation. It was he who had charge of the distribution of the many supplies that our Army sent in from the Philippines for the destitute Japanese people. Naturally, he was quite well known in Japan.

While I had been with my regiment at Fort Benjamin Harrison in Indiana he had been serving his second tour as the Military Attaché.

Colonel Burnett informed me that he knew of no suitable house available for us in Tokyo. The one he lived in was being preoccupied by the owner. The question before the house was what to do with the family until some house was found for rent. Then it was that Burnett told us he knew of a cottage for rent in the mountain summer resort of Karuizawa; that a language student, Captain Swift, now living in Karuizawa, would be glad to take us in until we could move into that house or elsewhere. So the decision was made that I would take the entire family to Karuizawa, settle them there and then return to Tokyo to take over my new duties.

So the next morning we took the train from the northern Ueno Station for the summer resort, Karuizawa. It was the 4th of July and it looked like our family for the first time would not be able to have our usual noisy celebration of that holiday.

The ride to Karuizawa took about four hours although it is less than 100 miles. The first sixty miles at least pass through a wide plain full of rice fields. The latter part of the trip our train went slowly up a steep grade through many tunnels, a tiresome and dirty experience. We disembarked at Shin Karuizawa where we were met by Captain Swift. He put us all in rikashas and away we went through the valley on top of Japan's main mountain range to the village of Karuizawa nearby, through that village to the northwest where we arrived at the Swift cottage in a pretty location with a splendid view of the active volcano of Asama.

The Swifts had several children and to our surprise the Captain had been able to secure the necessary wherewithal for plenty of noise so that evening we did, after all, have our celebration. That night we doubled up with the Swift family and the next day moved into a summer cottage in the foothills to the northeast of the village. This cottage we rented for the summer from a missionary family by the name of Pedley. It was completely furnished. I went over to the Mampei Hotel nearby where I was well known from my days there when a student. The owner promised to send me over some servants. This he did but we soon found that the cook insisted on feeding us so extravagantly that we had to get rid of him. No doubt, the bigger our bills for food, the bigger the squeeze for the cook.

Karuizawa was then a village of about 2,000 tradesmen surrounded by about the same number of foreigners and well-to-do Japanese living in foreign-style homes. The foreigners were largely missionaries, businessmen, and diplomats with their families.

Nearby was the active volcano Asama. It erupted more or less all the time. Often, it was necessary to carry an umbrella over one on the streets of Karuizawa to keep off the fine ashes that sifted down all around from the volcano. When a student, I had climbed it several times and thrown rocks into its crater full of boiling lava. Every summer climbers were injured by showers of stones thrown out at irregular intervals from its fiery crater. My first experience at the rim of the crater will never be forgotten. I arrived there before daylight. There was a full moon. Below us, stretching to the horizon, was a billowy mass of clouds silvery white from the rays of the moon. Before long, the moon began to set in the west while the sun was rising in the east. The combination of coloring effects on those clouds was most impressive and beyond description. As the sun rose higher one could see that the clouds were coming up. Soon they passed above us, and then the reflections from the fiery crater gave us more brilliant color pictures. And all this time, the earth rum-

41

bling, the crater was boiling just below us and occasionally throwing red hot rocks well above us.

There is another story I must tell of my student days in Karuizawa. My best friend among the other three American language students was Lieutenant George V. Strong. We had lived together in a pretty Japanese house opposite the home of the celebrated General Kuroki. But, in time, Strong had become enamored of the attractive daughter of the Danish Professor of Law at the Imperial University. And they married. The following summer, I was vacationing as usual at the Mampei Hotel just northeast of the village of Karuizawa and George and his wife, Gerda, were occupying a cottage just northwest of the village. Among the guests at the hotel were one British Captain from England, one British Captain of Indian troops, one French officer, and one German officer. Our Minister, Thomas J. O'Brien had a fine large summer cottage north of the village. Although the Minister spent most of his days in Tokyo, Mrs. O'Brien remained in the cottage throughout the summer.

It was that summer that we had the most awful ten days of rain that any place ever experienced. A prominent missionary claimed that he measured the rain fall and that during the first twenty-four hours, twenty-four inches fell; and that during the ten days, a total of fifty-six inches came down on that valley. Small mountain streams became raging torrents. Almost the entire valley was covered with rapidly flowing water. Due to the admixture of volcanic ash in the soil, a stream would quickly change its course often eating its way right through the yard of a fine home to the foundation of the house and then moving the house downstream or at least twisting it on its foundation. Part of one foreign hotel was washed away the first night, the water system of the village was destroyed, and some of the many railway tunnels nearby were much damaged so that the community was unable to get its daily supply of food by train.

The first day of that rain was like a continuous cloud burst. Never before or since have I seen such a down pour. Later in the afternoon I became alarmed concerning Mrs. O'Brien, who I knew was alone with her servants. So I went over to see her. Although her cottage was only about a half mile from my hotel and I had over my other clothes a good Army raincoat before I arrived I was thoroughly soaked to the skin. As I sloshed along, it seemed to me that the air was half rain. One seemed to breathe water.

Mrs. O'Brien made a big fuss over me, insisting that since it was so chilly I must take off everything, get into her husband's bathrobe, and sit by the fire while my clothing hung over chairs nearby to dry.

After warming and drying, I redressed and inspected the place. The cottage was on high ground just above the junction of and between two mountain streams. There in the foothills of the mountains the soil was thin and underneath was solid rock. There seemed to be little danger for Mrs. O'Brien at the time, so I hurried back to the hotel to see what else could be done. As I crossed the bridge adjoining her place the water of the raging stream was almost to the floor, and I learned later that soon after the bridge was washed away. Incidentally, I was never able to use that raincoat again. It had been completely ruined. Some chemical action appeared to have taken place. Thereafter it would not shed a teaspoonful of water.

The next morning an unusual view awaited us. The very small mountain stream which had meandered through that valley not far from our hotel had become a raging river. Half of the valley was covered with water.

Houses, trees, and other debris were scattered here and there.

I again decided to see how Mrs. O'Brien had fared. The stream on the hotel side of her grounds was now too wide, deep, and swift for me to attempt a crossing. My hope was that the stream on the opposite side of her grounds would be found to be passable. Moving toward the village, wading the many streams in the valley, I found that there was a deep stream running right down the main street of the village. So I had to make quite a detour around the village. Finally, after much difficulty, I came out on the bank of the stream that separated me from the grounds of the Minister's cottage. It was about forty feet wide, about three feet deep, and rushing madly between and over many big boulders. Perhaps it was a foolish thing to do but it seemed to me that someone should see that all was well with Mrs. O'Brien. So after a survey of possible crossings, I chose one and slowly waded in. Moving cautiously from boulder to boulder, sometimes wading, sometimes swimming, sometimes badly scared, I finally reached the other shore where my hands grasped some bushes which helped me up the steep bank out of the water. As I turned to take a parting glance at my late enemy, to my surprise, there stood all alone on the high bank from which I had just come, the attractive daughter of a Canadian missionary whose home was near there. That should have been perhaps the beginning of a romance, but sorry my reader, it just did not work out that way.

So my second call on Mrs. O'Brien was accomplished. She was safe on that high rocky point, so I returned by the same long route around the village to my hotel.

At the hotel there awaited me the interesting news that Lieutenant Strong, my friend, fellow Language Student, and classmate at West Point, had been placed in charge of the valley.

It appears that while I had been circling the village and calling on Mrs. O'Brien, a group of foreigners had assembled at the upper end of the village to discuss the serious situation. The story goes that while the crowd was stating its troubles and arguing about what could be done, Lieutenant Strong climbed up on a stump and announced that if they would promise to obey him he would be willing to take charge of the situation. Incidentally, Strong was the lowest ranking member of the American Legation personnel, but he had plenty of ability and no end of confidence in himself. Strong's proposal was accepted by the crowd with enthusiasm. He wasted not a minute in selecting an office, organizing a working force, seizing the food supply, rationing it, and sending a mule team over the mountains for more supplies.

He announced that he wanted a volunteer force for much needed manual labor. About one hundred responded. They were composed of foreign diplomats, missionaries, and businessmen. One lone Japanese joined up. He had been educated in America and was then stopping at the Mampei Hotel. The British Captain of Indian troops and I offered our services so Strong divided the group into two platoons and placed the captain in charge of one and me in charge of the other. The British Captain from England and the French and German officers remained aloof.

Well, for ten days we worked that group hard building dams, saving homes, saving personnel from homes surrounded by water, constructing a new water system for the village, and building new bridges. Most of the gang had never known what it was to work with their hands but they were willing. We had few tools. Improvisation was the rule. That daughter of the Canadian missionary brought us some Japanese tools which she secured by her own efforts, I suppose from Japanese families—she spoke excellent Japanese. She and Lieutenant Strong's young wife kept us supplied with hot coffee.

It was an interesting experience handling those men, teaching them how to fell a tree, make bridges, and dams, and dig ditches. They seemed to enjoy working with their hands in the water and mud. Probably they felt like heroes. I know it was difficult for me to get away from that work even after Strong had dismissed us. My platoon still wanted to do things that might be useful, and they insisted on my being present and in charge of the work. It amused me that they should be so impressed by my knowledge of how to use an axe, saw, hammer, shovel, etc., how to dig ditches and construct dams and bridges. I often heard them say, "Learned it at West Point." Well, I let West Point have the credit but most of the know-how that I made use of there had been learned as a boy on a Midwest farm. Leadership, the willingness to take responsibility, those things West Point had taught me and I found much use for them during those ten days.

Lieutenant Strong lived to be a Major General and was in charge of Army Intelligence in Washington during World War II.

Now back to 1929. After about a week, I left my family comfortably and happily established in their new home and returned to Tokyo to prepare for the new duties for which my government had sent me to Japan.

V

Taking Over from My Predecessor

Returning to Tokyo I took a room at the Imperial Hotel, the one that was built by Frank Lloyd Wright of Chicago, the one with its unusual architecture, but which stood up all through that terrible earthquake of 1923, which destroyed all of Yokohama and large parts of Tokyo also. Now, I was ready to go to work as the Military Attaché.

The next morning I was up bright and early. It was to be a big day for me, every minute of which I expected to find interesting. After a good breakfast I strolled out the front entrance to get a taxi. There I saw one lone rikashaman. Just what I wanted, so I engaged him to take me to the office of Colonel Burnett at 32 Dote Sanbancho, Kojimachiku, about three miles. I enjoyed that ride around the moat of the Emperor's palace grounds. It carried me back to my student days when nearly everyone went everywhere in rikashas. It was a bright sunny day. As I rolled along, familiar places met my eye and I noted the changes that had taken place.

Upon arrival at Colonel Burnett's, to my surprise, I found that his office was in a building in the garden of what was known as the Gardner Home, a place with which I was most familiar as a student. In fact, that family still owned it and had rented it to the Burnetts who lived in the house. The Burnetts, the servants, and the office personnel laughed heartily when they noted my means of travel. They said no one ever rode in rikashas anymore. They were right for that was the only rikasha seen by me in that city. I found that everyone walked, pedaled some type of bicycle or tricycle, or rode in a Ford taxi.

The Burnetts were almost ready to pull out. Their household goods were largely packed with the crates and boxes piled high here and there in their rooms. It was the end of Colonel Burnett's second four-year tour as the Military Attaché at Tokyo. It seemed evident that they were not happy to be leaving Japan for perhaps the last time for they had both come to be fond of that country and its people. They were well known throughout Japan. The fact that he had been the dispenser of the American Army supplies after the 1923 earthquake made him favorably known throughout the land but especially well in and around Tokyo and Yokohama.

Incidentally, the Burnetts had lost all their belongings in the fire following that earthquake including many valuable art pieces collected during nine years of living in Japan.

Colonel Burnett introduced me to his office personnel. Among them was his confidential secretary, Miss MacMahon. I had known her when she worked in the Military Intelligence Division in Washington. Her father had been a General and her brother was then an officer of the Army.

Burnett showed me his records, his files, and talked some about the handling of the finances of the office, but to my surprise, he told me nothing about how to secure information for the government. In Washington, there had been the same lack of advice or instructions as to how to operate. The latter is easily understood for there was no

School of Intelligence and among the personnel in the Intelligence Division probably not one had ever been a Military Attaché. Our government was still very inexperienced in dealing with hard boiled old foreign governments with their long-trained diplomats and intelligence forces. Our policies were of course the direct result of our form of government and the attitude of our people toward such matters. Our location in the world and our great resources had saved us so far.

Having had five years in the Orient and a tour in the Military Intelligence Division in Washington, I was much better prepared than the officers going to European or South American countries. They must have had a lot to learn. About the only thing they seriously tried to teach me during the two-week stop in Washington concerned the accounting for the funds they expected to give me for various purposes.

In a storeroom, Burnett showed me a large supply of whiskey, wines, and liquors that he had imported from Europe. These, I purchased from him, as I did also a beautiful silver cocktail set including a tray, shaker, and twelve cups.

They bragged much about their servants and asked that we take them over, which I promised to do. I had lunch with them that day.

But I begged off when it came to buying Mrs. Burnett's set of beautiful wine glasses at $125 for already inquiry had informed me that I could secure a quite passable set for about $20.

As stated before, the house in which the Burnetts were living I had known as a student. The Gardners had three attractive daughters who knew well the daughters of the high ranking Japanese families. They often asked me to tea and to dance with those Japanese girls, an unusual privilege for a young foreigner at that time. This led to my being able to call at the homes of some of those young girls, also most unusual for those days.

They informed me that the Gardner house would not be available to us, so much of my time was taken up for the next month in a search for a building in which not only my family could live and entertain, but in which there was room for a large office.

You see at that time there was no building in Tokyo owned by our government for use of the Embassy. The old one where I had lived much of my tour as a student and attaché of the Legation had been burned during the earthquake of 1923. We still held the grounds but that was all. The ambassador and his staff occupied offices in a commercial building in the center of the business district. The large personnel of the embassy rented quarters anywhere they could find them.

During this time I spent much of each day pouring over the office files, especially those reports of Colonel Burnett written recently, which I did not see in Washington or in the Philippines. There was many an hour of conversation with the Colonel exchanging views and impressions about Japan's Army, people, etc. He took me to the American Club, the Tokyo Club, the Tokyo Tennis Club. As we went about, he was continually introducing me to important Americans, Europeans, and Japanese.

My official calling cards were secured in a hurry. Then it took much time to go about the city and leave them on all the Japanese government officials of importance to me, at the various diplomatic missions. At certain places my card only was left but at other places Gwynneth's card was left with mine, and it was all a serious matter. A mistake might cause a misunderstanding that would be annoying to have to explain and straighten out. Some diplomats and officials of some foreign countries can at times be most sensitive to any apparent or even most unintentional slight or oversight. When calling on the Princes we were required to wear full-dress uniform. At their official residences we were admitted to a room where we were expected to sign a book for visitors. At none of the official calls did we see the person on whom we were calling. It was simply the customary way of announcing to them that you were there for duty. Within a few days those calls would be returned. Officials usually sent a subordinate to deposit their cards in the box at your door or gate. Then you were assured that official Tokyo knew of your presence.

Sometime in August, the Burnetts went to Nikko to await the arrival of their transport. So from that time I was largely on my own.

VI
Our First Home

About the first of September a foreign type house in No.
13 Reinanzaka became vacant. It was owned by an American real estate firm. They rented it to me for $200 a
month. It had seven rooms; on the first floor, one very
large dining room, two medium-sized rooms, an inclosed
veranda overlooking a small garden, a hall, and a very
small kitchen. The second floor was the same except for
the kitchen. It was steam heated inadequately, by a furnace that was outside the house near the kitchen. The
small garden was surrounded by a high bamboo fence.
The house was in a compound with four other foreign-type houses occupied by the American Naval
Attaché, the First Secretary of the American Embassy, a
representative of the Associated Press, and an Englishman who was the head of an insurance company. Such
compounds were to be found here and there in Tokyo like
little foreign oases in the vast Japanese city.

For my office, I took over the large dining room, and
we filled it, for there was my assistant, Lieutenant
Cranford, my stenographer, Miss MacMahon, one clerk
(Hawaiian), one translator (Japanese) and one messenger (Formosan). In addition, there were a large safe and
extensive office files. My family were still in Karuizawa.

Now, having a house, I wanted a home and for that

our household goods were necessary so I began a search for them. Before long, I learned that they had been in Tokyo for a long time and had been placed for storage in a storeroom under the elevated railway that connected the Shimbashi and Ueno Stations. After considerable difficulty with red tape our goods were delivered at the door of our new home. Then I took off my coat and plunged into the task of unboxing and uncrating it all, an American boxcar load of it.

Our property had been handled at least thirteen times in its trip from Fort Benjamin Harrison, but to my surprise there had been no great amount of damage. This was probably due to my timely repairs at San Francisco and Manila. However, a few things had been smashed and a few things needed repairs. I submitted a claim for reimbursement for damages to the War Department and the items were all approved with the exception of one for six wine glasses. The board of officers that had acted on my claim had disallowed those wine glasses and made the remark in their report that wine glasses were an unnecessary item of an officer's household property. The fact is that there was not one item on that list that would be used any more than those wine glasses. Both at luncheons and dinners both Orientals and Europeans expected wine to be served. I was thankful for the reimbursement for the other losses and even appreciated their disapproval of the wine glasses for it always made a good dinner story. One might well suspect that some officer on that board had a sense of humor.

And how did we make use of our new house? As I have said, the office took over the very large dining room at one end of the first floor. The middle room became the dining room and the end room near the entrance became the living room. On the second floor; the very large room over the office was turned over to the three daughters for their bedroom. My son was put out on the enclosed veranda. The middle room over the dining room was used as a second floor living and work room, while Gwynneth and I took as our bedroom the end room over the first floor living room. So we were now well set for the beginning of real work.

VII
Suggestions to the War Department

One of the first things I did after settling myself at my new desk in Reinanzaka was to send two suggestions to the War Department. These were based on my own experience as I traveled from our own country to Japan. I had spent over two months on that trip, most of it being on our transports. It might well be considered a fine opportunity for rest provided one were in need of it. But, to me, it seemed to be a decided waste of the average officer's time. It was the third time I had crossed the Pacific by transport and the conditions were found to be the same on all three trips.

The first suggestion concerned the libraries on the transports. The second suggestion related to our stops at Panama, San Francisco, Honolulu, and Manila.

With reference to the libraries, they had always contained practically nothing but cheap novels. With reference to our stops, officers, when they went ashore, were entirely on their own as far as learning anything from a military standpoint concerning that section of the world.

My idea in general was that such a trip would be a grand opportunity for an officer to improve his knowledge of our defense installations in Panama, San Francisco, and in our island possessions, and to increase our general knowledge of our distant possessions, neighboring countries and especially of the islands of the Caribbean Sea and the Pacific Ocean. My claim was that we had so few professional officers that all should be taught as much as possible because anyone of them might find himself in a future war in a position requiring a knowledge of some or all of those places.

So I recommended that all transports be equipped with books relating to the West Indies, Panama, San Francisco and vicinity, the Hawaiian Islands, the Philippines, Pacific Islands in general, Formosa, China, and Japan. And I suggested that the Commanding Officer of a transport should encourage the reading of certain books before the arrival at a port and might well detail certain officers to lecture on countries they were passing and on countries they were visiting before arrival.

My other recommendation was that upon arrival of the transport at Panama, San Francisco, Honolulu, and Manila, officer guides and transportation should meet the transport for the purpose of taking the traveling officers in groups to visit all the defenses in that vicinity that were not top secret.

As far as I know, my carefully prepared written suggestions produced no good results whatsoever.

VIII

My New Situation

Let me now describe the situation in which I found myself as the new Military Attaché.

Colonel Burnett, my predecessor, had sailed for the United States. There was no ambassador at that time. There was a large Embassy force, however, headed by Edwin Neville, who as Counselor became the Chargé d'Affaires. As I have mentioned before, the old Legation buildings had been burned in the earthquake of 1923. The Embassy offices were in a modern type building in the central business section of the city and the personnel were scattered, living in all parts of the city wherever they could find passable quarters.

Mr. Neville I knew well for he had been a student interpreter at the same time I had been a student officer attached to the Legation back in the years 1908–1911. In fact, I had lived with him for some time. He was a rough diamond, rather ordinary in appearance, a graduate of Michigan University, a constant reader of history, both ancient and modern, especially military history and he remembered everything he read. After a few drinks at a stag dinner, he could get up and bring down the house with a perfect rendition of that stirring oration entitled "Why Change the Name of Arkansas." He did know Japan and the Japanese.

Edwin had a wife known as Betsy. She was the salt of the earth. Not attractive in looks, she had everything else. She slaved for Eddie and their two young sons. She was a real leader, not only among the American Embassy group but among the American business group as well. Everyone liked her including the Japanese.

Included in the Embassy force was the Naval Attaché, the Commercial Attaché, the First Secretary, the Second Secretary, the Third Secretary, and quite a force of clerks both American and Japanese. There were also the Consul General and his staff and later came the newly established Trade Commissioner.

The Naval Attaché had his one office assistant and several young student officers. I, as the Military Attaché, had one officer assistant, a clerical force of three and one messenger. In addition, under my guidance were from four to ten student officers most of whom lived in Tokyo. That new home of ours was none too large for on an average day the personnel in that house totaled fifteen; the family of six, the office force of five, and the servant group of four.

Soon we settled down to the interesting life of a Military Attaché in a country supposed to be friendly to ours. The usual morning for me was four hours of work at my desk. Often I was invited out for lunch. The early afternoons were usually spent in the office. The late afternoons were taken up by the making of official or private calls, attending diplomatic teas, or cocktail parties, or in exercise on the courts of the Tokyo Tennis Club not far away. It was found worthwhile to drop in often just before the dinner hour at the Tokyo Club and join the big round table there where could be found an interesting and important group of Japanese foreign officials and businessmen, chatting and throwing the bones for another drink.

For dinner, we were usually invited out or had guests of our own. Even after dinner, special parties were not uncommon.

IX

My Official Duties

Bear in mind that I am now writing about the *first half* of my tour in Japan as the Military Attaché. It lasted from July 1929 to September 1931.

Military Attachés are sent to foreign countries for just one reason—to secure information of value to our War Department. This information may concern the country in which the Military Attaché is resident or it may concern some country adjacent or near the country where he is living. That information is not necessarily strictly military in character. Far from it. The Military Intelligence Division divided such information into Combat, Economic, Political, Social and Geographic. Combat included the strictly military information covering the organization, training, equipment, supply, and morale of the Army. Economic information dealt with the nation's resources and the ability of the country to manufacture war weapons and supplies. Political information had to do with the country's internal politics, its political parties, its leaders, its probable stand in world affairs in the future. For the Social file we were expected to make a deep study of the people, their customs, their national character and reactions, and their feelings toward Americans. Under Geographic we reported on the climate, the terrain of different parts, and were always on the lookout for the latest and best maps.

Now in the Military Intelligence Division there was a large index that listed in logical order under the five main divisions mentioned in the preceding paragraph in great detail the various subjects on which information was desired. Each military attaché office had a copy of that index and I suspect that one was in Manila, Honolulu, and the Panama Canal Zone.

Each foreign country of any importance was represented in the Military Intelligence Division by one or more officers and one or more confidential clerks. Their duty was the constant collection, evaluation, and dissemination of the information on the country or countries on which they worked. This information came from Military Attachés, Naval Attachés, Commercial Attachés, Consular Officers, Embassies, Legations, American travelers and residents upon their return to the United States, and the leading newspapers of our own country.

After the information on any subject had been evaluated and properly written up, it then became known as "intelligence," was given a heading and number in accord with the Master Index, and then placed for file in big loose leaf binders where it could readily be found by officers of the Intelligence Division, the War Plans Division, and the students and instructors of the War College.

When I was in charge of the Far Eastern Section in Washington around 1925, we had sufficient personnel but this was apparently reduced from time to time until it was ridiculously insufficient. For instance, when I returned to Washington from Japan in 1933, there was but one officer working on Japan and he had but one typist, and that for part-time only. It is difficult to understand why that section was permitted to run down in the face of all the trouble into which we appeared to be heading.

The first indication of the reduction in activity of that

section came to me shortly after I settled down to work in Japan. At that time the Division sent me instructions that thereafter the final writing of all intelligence for Japan for file in the War Department would be largely my responsibility. That my reports would be made with that idea in view. That my reports would be filed as received. This increased my work and responsibility greatly for now I had to search for and collect information under each and all digest holdings, hold each until enough information was secured for me to make a proper evaluation, and then with great care shape it into pages for the files of the Intelligence Division. Of course, in the meantime, any important information had to be forwarded immediately, thus in many cases the same facts were reported twice, first in the rough as it were and later in a finished form.

In other words, my office took over a large part of the work that formerly, and properly so, had belonged in the Far Eastern Section at Washington. And I say properly with emphasis for there they had on their desk before them not only my reports but information from many sources not available to me. However, the new plan probably worked satisfactorily from the standpoint of the War Department since they had reduced the personnel there. It is the first time the plan would have worked, for the fact is it was the first time in our history that there had been sent to Japan an officer who had been four years a student in Japan and had had a tour in the Military Intelligence Division.

This new plan compelled me to continually search the Master Index and our intelligence files for subjects the write-ups of which were evidently not up to date. When such a subject was found, I would start a series of actions contemplated to get the latest information on that subject, file it temporarily as it came in; from time to time get it out and mull it over like a Chinese puzzle until one day I would find it making sense. Then it would be written up as a new article, three copies sent to the Division and one copy kept in our files. My recollection is that of those copies sent to the Division, they sent one to the Commanding General of the Philippines and one to the Military Attaché in China when the subject was of possible interest to those offices.

As stated previously, the mission given me by the Chief of the Military Intelligence Section as I left Washington was to study and report on how best to bomb Japan. This I knew would take much time and study before a report of any real value could be written. As far as I know, that was the first time anyone had been given that assignment. That mission was kept in my mind from the first. My travels were planned with it in mind. To make such a report would require a thorough knowledge of the geography and climate of the country, its railroads, water systems, hydro-electric plants, bridges, great productive centers, airfields, and air units. In my travels by rail I sat much of the time on the rear platform of the last car observing everything of military interest. In travel by boat I was on deck if permitted or looking through a porthole if possible.

As soon as we arrived in Japan I realized that my ability to handle the Japanese language had suffered much due to disuse during the seventeen years of my absence from that country. So every day of my first year as Military Attaché I tried to work in a review of some of my old textbooks and of course took advantage of every opportunity to talk to Japanese in their own language.

One of the first things I did after sitting down at my own desk was to look into the funds provided for the office of the Military Attaché, the amounts, how allotted in detail and how they had to be accounted for. I soon found that the situation was very unsatisfactory from my standpoint. I had been told in Washington that there would be a certain substantial sum made available to me in addition to my regular monthly pay for such use as I might wish to make of it. There were two uses which I naturally had in mind. One to help me secure information for my government, the other to assist me in the necessary entertaining that went with the job. Actually entertaining was one way of securing information.

Now I found that all this money was tied down into certain definite little pigeonholes, so much for an office, so much for the upkeep of a government-owned car, so much for a garage for the government-owned car, a definite sum for stationery, another small amount for newspapers and periodicals, etc. The money was there, but not in the way I wanted to use it. For instance, the man from whom I rented the house insisted that I pay him by the month in advance by one check, and refused to be a party to any plan of splitting up the rent, part for the house less one room, and part for the one room which was my office. So, if I kept my papers straight as I would back in the United States, there was little possibility of ever being able to use the money allotted for an office.

At first, I had the old decrepit government car turned over by Colonel Burnett. Soon, however, I found it advisable to sell it for the government and I had sent out to me a secondhand car purchased for me from private funds. So then I could not make use of the money for a garage for there was no government car used by me. And so it went with all that money sent me. Only now and then could I used it as allotted and be strictly honest in my accounting.

None of that money had been allotted for securing information or for entertaining. Later, as I recall, they did send me a small amount for entertaining but with a string tied to it that it could not be used in entertaining Americans. There again was the usefulness of the fund restricted. The fact is that often certain American businessmen can be the source of a great deal of important information especially in the economic, political, and social lines.

I recall how when I was a student officer in Japan, one of the Military Attachés of that time took us into his confidence and showed us how impossible it was for him to make use of certain funds sent him from Washington and be honest in accounting for it in the way required by the War Department. At that time, he made quite a fight with the assistance of other Military Attachés in other parts of the world to have the accounting simplified and made more adaptable for use in a foreign country. He had absolutely no success. I recall his showing us a letter from the War Department turning down his suggestion but in the envelope was an unsigned typed statement on a slip of paper suggesting how he might by irregular methods make use of the money and account for it.

His difficulties were no surprise to me, for I had gone through that when as a new Second Lieutenant the Commanding Officer of the Legation Guard in Peking, China, had made me the Quartermaster and Commissary for those troops. I almost sweat blood over what I had to do in order to get those troops fed, and at the same time, submit the voluminous papers that were required by the War Department. For instance, I asked for bids for the supply of sugar for our personnel of two hundred. The lowest bid and the best sugar came from a certain British firm. But the representative of that firm would not sign our elaborate vouchers with their lengthy instructions thereon.

Said his firm forbid his signing foreign government vouchers. If we wanted sugar, we must use his forms. Well, my instructions said I must take the lowest bid if the quality was satisfactory. Other foreigners refused to sign their names in the way required by our War Department. How we got around that obstacle seems funny now but it was not then.

Now as the Military Attaché, I realized that I was in a bad spot for I had to account for every penny and certify as to how it was spent and of course, the reports to the War Department had to show that the money was spent as allotted originally by it.

What was I to do? If I were wholly correct and exact in my financial reports as I had always been when on duty in the United States, there would be little or no money available for carrying out my real objective—the securing of information. If I made such a decision, I might as well so inform the War Department and suggest return to the United States, for it is probable that they would not leave me there long with my big family and no extra financial help. An early recall would certainly be bad on my reputation in the Army. Brother officers would suspect misconduct or inability to handle the job. The War Department certainly would not want me to broadcast the facts. On the other hand, I was convinced that the Military Intelligence Division really expected me to juggle those funds for the best interests of the government.

Well, finally after much worry and study, I deliberately decided to adjust my funds so that I could use them to the best advantage for the purposes for which I believed they had been given me. The funds thus secured I took personally and spent as I felt was best. But I kept a detailed account of my own under lock and key as to how the money was actually used. Of course, my office clerical force had to know of my decision for they prepared my financial reports.

It was a ridiculous set up forced upon me by the government. My assistant, Lieutenant Cranford, was needed for work on securing economical and political information, but most of his time was taken up with office financial matters. Most of the time of the clerks was also spent in the preparation of financial papers. The combined salaries of those clerks greatly exceeded the sum of money they were accounting for.

It is an interesting fact to note that the only criticism I received from Washington on my work in Tokyo concerned errors in my finance papers. As I have written before, it takes an expert to handle the complicated financial returns now expected by the Finance Department of the Army. The situation was really funny at times. We would receive a long official letter from Washington calling our attention to some small error when in fact, the whole return was incorrect and known by all in the office to be so.

Did the Naval Attaché have the same financial difficulties as I did? Not at all. His only personnel in his office was one Petit Officer assistant who incidentally was never overworked and the Naval Attaché always had time for golf in the afternoons. His office had a lump sum for which he accounted in a very simple way. In contrast, I had an office force of five, and between the finance problem and me, they were kept busy. When we might have two hundred abstracts and vouchers to turn in at the end of a quarter, some quite complicated, the Naval Attaché would have but one abstract and perhaps a dozen simple vouchers.

This system was, I believe, partly law, partly inefficiency of the War Department, and partly Civil Service keeping all possible jobs for their personnel. But why did the War Department put up with it when the Navy did not? That, I cannot answer.

I think it was in 1931 that our office force heard that an inspector was coming up from the Philippines to look over all finance accounts of our government in Tokyo. My personnel were frightened but I soon calmed them by stating that in the first place, I believed the inspector would have instructions to leave us alone, and in the second place, if he did come to our office I would refuse to let him see anything until I received orders from the War Department to permit him that privilege; and if those orders were received, I would take the responsibility for the whole matter.

The inspector went through everyone's accounts in the Embassy, then we heard he was in the office of the Commercial Attaché, later in the Consul General's office, and we continued to wait uneasily. Finally came word that he was on his way back to Manila, and then a sigh of relief went up from our office. We learned later that he had not visited the office of the Naval Attaché, but I suspect that the Naval Captain could have shown his accounts without any embarrassment.

Now, why have I recounted here all this financial difficulty? The answer is that I have hopes that it may move someone with power and influence to start action for a change. A young officer coming out of West Point where he has been trained that everything which appears on paper above his signature must be an absolute fact is terribly shocked when he finds himself in a position where for the good of his own country he must resort to incorrect accounts as I did in both Peking and Tokyo.

One of my important responsibilities was the handling of the group of young Army officers attached to the

Embassy. They were detailed for a period of four years to study the Japanese language. That was too long to study hard on one difficult subject like that. I tried to have them returned to the States for one year of duty after two years in Japan, but I was never able to accomplish it. I also fought for a broadening of their studies to include the Japanese Army, Japan's history, geography, customs, etc. In this, I was successful in that I did arrange for their being attached to the Japanese Army as an observer for six months, and was permitted to arrange a schedule of study for them that was much broader than formerly. Every six months they were required to undergo an examination to determine their progress. This was supervised and partly conducted by me.

In my experience, there was no trouble about getting the officer to study his subjects with energy. They were a well-selected group not noted for laziness. My trouble was in keeping them from studying too much. They were all prone to spend too many hours a day at the Japanese language without taking the necessary exercise and recreation. Some of the officers would have periods when they were completely worn out mentally, almost nervous wrecks. A number had internal physical trouble which was probably caught from their food. Sometimes it was the wife of one of them who needed some guidance. But generally speaking, they were a fine group of young officers and I have no doubt that they gave most useful service during the late war.

X

The Production of Intelligence

A good Intelligence Officer has three words with which he is very familiar. They are collection, evaluation, and dissemination. Information must first be collected or secured. Then it is evaluated and written up. It is then known as Intelligence. But it is still of use to no one until it has been disseminated or distributed to persons and offices where it will be made use of.

In the Military Intelligence Division in Washington much use was made of bright intelligent young women who could do research and write well. Some of them had been with the division for many years and those often knew more about the details about a country than the General Staff Officer over them. But the Military Attaché does his own preparation of reports and they are usually the kind that require much thought, not the sort of thing where one can call a stenographer and dash it off in a few minutes.

Now, how is this information secured? There are many sources available to the average Military Attaché. In a truly friendly country, the task of securing information is usually very easy—a simple one. But in a country unfriendly to us the job of securing information may become a very difficult one. Japan was such a country. Its Army leaders were not friendly to us. Every effort was made to keep us from securing information of value. Almost everything pertaining to the Army and Navy is considered by them to be secret. In the United States, almost any book published for the Army can be purchased for a small sum from the public printer. The Japanese Military Attaché in Washington could even buy them himself, as he could also almost any map in existence in this country. All that is impossible in Japan. It is a major problem to secure any book on the organization or training of their Army.

Some of the sources of information in Japan were:

Newspapers, magazines, books
Observation
Conversations
Inspections
Travel
Official requests to the Japanese War Department
Other foreign Military Attachés
Brought in by my assistant in the office or by the language students

A Military Attaché may subscribe to any non-secret publication in Japan. It is not unusual to find information in them which, when placed with other seemingly unimportant statements secured elsewhere, do add up to something of importance. At the office was one intelligent Japanese employee whom we used as interpreter and translator. Each advanced student read one or more Japanese papers and periodicals. As part of their instruction they were required to submit translations they knew or suspected would be of interest to our office. Sometimes they were given definite assignments for translation.

As for observation as a source, all of us officers in Japan were expected to keep our eyes open for information. We observed in detail any troops we might have the good fortune to see on the march. We noted their discipline, their morale, their physical condition, the number of their unit, their equipment. At the yearly Imperial Review in Tokyo and the Fall Grand Imperial Maneuvers, there was always something of value picked up.

Information secured from conversation ordinarily was under doubt. It usually had to be tested with other similar information. But often important facts were derived from this source. It might be from a personal conversation or from overhearing a conversation. Even the secretive Japanese officer has been known to become indiscreet in his cups or to brag too much. And even capable foreign businessmen at times would forget their caution and tell of their success in selling certain products to the Japanese government. Sometimes a Japanese official at a social affair would deliberately tell me something he wanted our government to know. Often foreign diplomats and Military Attachés would do likewise.

Inspections were made as frequently as the situation seemed to justify. To make an inspection, we had to obtain permission of the Japanese War Department to visit the place in question. You see in our intelligence files we had a description and often a map of each military school, post, arsenal, and supply base. There were many of these. From time to time, we would have reason to believe that our write-up on a certain establishment was out of date. In asking permission to visit a place, I often requested that I be permitted to take with me my assistant and perhaps one language student. These requests had to be made in writing formally. Sometimes the request was granted, and sometimes it was not granted. If granted, a date and hour for the visit would be stated by the Japanese. Before going, I would call the other officers who were going with me into my office to explain the situation, showing them the then present write-up and telling them what changes I expected to find. Each officer would be told what he should try to learn from his officer guide, and would be allotted certain portions of the grounds and buildings to observe in detail. As soon as we returned to the office, we would sit down and together make out a new map of the place from memory, and we would all make lists of any information of interest we had obtained. From these notes and a study of the old article on the subject, I personally would prepare the new report and map for the files.

In our travels, we kept on the alert to observe any troops it was possible to see on the train, at the stations, or on the march on a nearby road. We were always on the lookout for new types of equipment. One also took advantage of his being in any new city to obtain the much decorated commercial map sold to civilians by the curio stores. They were often sufficiently accurate to be worthwhile. Personally, I made quite a collection, which helped me in the preparation of my important report on how to bomb Japan.

Occasionally a letter would come to me from the Military Intelligence Division with instructions to secure certain information from the Japanese War Department. This, I would request by letter. They were terribly slow in replying. It was evident to me that they wished to discourage any attempt to secure information that way. It usually took a couple of personal calls at their office before I could get a reply out of them and then those replies usually contained little information on the subject in question. I had heard that our Military Intelligence Division was very helpful to the Japanese Military Attaché in

Washington, so I wrote them suggesting that they tighten up and treat the Japanese Military Attaché the same way I was being treated. The reply was more than unsatisfactory. It said that they were proud of the efficiency with which their office secured the necessary information and replied to the Japanese and other foreign Military Attachés without delay. And they suggested that if I would mix with the Japanese officers more informally, I would find that they would treat me the same way. Not much cooperation there. The officer who wrote that answer probably had never been in Japan and knew almost nothing about the Japanese military type.

The foreign officer with whom I became best acquainted while in Tokyo was the French Military Attaché. Finally, he and I arranged to give each other copies of important reports which we had prepared. Sometimes when he knew I was working on a certain important report, he would say that at present he had nothing of equal importance to exchange but that he knew of a certain study in the military files in Paris that he would have sent to Washington in exchange. Those French studies were made up by skilled professional officers and were usually very worth having. This arrangement worked very well for us, but the Japanese were much displeased by it. Several times they made some sarcastic remark to me about that good French friend of mine. I never was able to arrange any exchanges of information with a British Military Attaché. They were always very reticent, evidently desiring to play their own game. The British Ambassador and his wife were much more cordial and the Ambassador often went out of his way to exchange ideas with me. I thought that sometimes he tried to influence our Ambassador through me.

The Polish Military Attaché was very cordial, as was

also his assistant. They were officers of much experience in the World War and the Russian-Polish war following. No doubt they were keeping watch on the activities of the Russians. But I never got much out of them. The Italian was not much of a mixer at least among Anglo Saxons. Just once I got something of importance from him. Will tell you about that later on.

The Spanish speaking Military Attachés I did not know well. Also, I felt they would have little to impart of value to us. In fact, we had the largest military force in Japan and believed that we had more information than any of the others.

My assistant, Lieutenant Cranford, brought in much valuable information especially along economic and political lines. He was a natural born mixer, enjoyed club life, and so had many contacts among the foreign businessmen, and even some good Japanese contacts.

Now and then, a student would come in with something worthwhile. I encouraged them to travel and to live in different parts of the country. Incidentally, when I was in charge of the Far Eastern Section of the Military Intelligence Division in Washington, I persuaded the authorities to exchange Language Officers with Japan for the purpose of attaching them to troops. My argument for this exchange was that the Japanese could find out all about our forces very easily but it was very difficult for us to learn about theirs, due to the difference in secretiveness. We could lose nothing and gain a lot. It was quite a Spartan life lived by our student officers when with Japanese troops. But it was an unusual experience that gave them an idea of Japanese soldiers and officers that could not be gained in any other way. And when they completed their tour with a Japanese unit, they would submit a lengthy report, which generally was of considerable value.

XI
Social Life

At first it occurred to me to write about the official side of the social life and then about the social life with our friends, but upon further thought it seemed better not to attempt any such division, for like it or not, most of our social life was due to our position in the Embassy. Even among our closest friends, who were American business people and tourists it would be difficult to say positively that they were friends without a purpose back of the friendship.

Remember again I am writing about conditions during the first period of our stay in Japan from July 1929 to September 1931. During this time our social contacts with the Japanese officials, and that includes the State, Army, and Navy groups, were most satisfactory. There was little evidence, if any, of animosity toward us. The liberal elements of Japan were in power. The country had in general a very good constitution. There was the god-like Emperor, and a Parliament with its House of Peers and its House of Commons. Their members were elected by the people. No doubt big business pulled the strings largely under cover behind the scenes as it were. Leading politicians, statesmen, and businessmen were peacefully inclined. They believed that Japan could go farther by use of her commercial advantages than she could by war. Baron Shidehara, then Minister of Foreign Affairs, once said to me when we had been talking about the aggressive Army group, that "it is a mistake to think that we can prosper by the use of brute strength against our neighbors. When a nation makes use of force to expand rapidly it attracts against itself the united strength of many other nations and generally ends up in disaster. I believe in growing great and strong through commercial methods, and I know that I am just as patriotic as those aggressive Army officers," or words to that effect.

It should be borne in mind that Japan from about the twelfth century until around 1868 had been a feudal country. Even today much of that feudalism remains in the minds of the people. That feudalistic society built up, especially among the military group, a type of super patriot. They were also quite common among the civilians. The latter were often organized into secret underground societies. These secret organizations could exercise great power through their willingness to assassinate a political leader who refused to listen to them.

But during the period about which I am now writing, the aggressive super patriot was not in power. He was being held in check. The Army and to some degree the Navy, were not receiving much of the budget. I know myself that at that time the Army had inferior weapons and supplies in general, inferior both in quantity and quality. The Army officers were poorly paid and greatly overworked. It was quite evident that the Army officers smarted under what they considered unfair treatment. They were even then quietly planning for a change to be brought about by force if necessary. But in spite of the small funds allotted the Army, they managed to keep their conscription, which made possible a standing Army of 250,000 and about two million in reserve. That Army was well disciplined and well trained in the use of its poor equipment. It had given a good account of itself on the march to Peking in 1900 and in the Russo-Japan War of 1904.

There were undoubtedly many Japanese in important positions who wished their country to be on the most friendly relations with the United States. A fine appearing group met annually for a big dinner for graduates of American colleges. Americans met with them. A strong organization was the American-Japan Society, which met once a month at least. A number of prominent Japanese both in and out of official life belonged to this society and took an active part in making it a success. Its President was Prince Tokugawa, the last of the great Shogun family that had ruled Japan for over two hundred years before the arrival of Admiral Perry and his ships of war. He was an able man with a very likable personality. I must tell you an incident that took place one day at the Imperial Hotel at a luncheon given by the America-Japan Society for some important American visitors. Prince Tokugawa was the toastmaster for that occasion. Seated next to me was an attractive middle-aged woman, the mother of one of our Vice-Consuls in Harbin. She was enroute to visit her son. I had been telling her what a fine man the Prince was. She had said to me, "I cannot believe that any such man exists among the Japanese." Hardly had she made that remark than the Prince arose and told us that he regretted very much that he would have to leave us now as he just had time to reach the Diet Building in time for the opening of the House of Peers. Incidentally, he was the ranking member and so the presiding officer of that body. He left his chair and as he passed in our rear on his way out to his waiting motor car he stopped and leaning over my shoulder said, "Colonel McIlroy, how is that lovely wife of yours and that new baby?" Mrs. McIlroy was not present that day for she had only recently added a fine young daughter to the McIlroy family. From his conversation, it was evident that he had just talked with someone who knew our family situation. As he passed on, the American mother said to me, "I take back what I said a moment ago. It is remarkable that such a busy man as he must be should think of and take the time for such a good gesture of friendship," or words to that effect.

Later on, they made me the American Secretary of that America-Japan Society. It gave me an opportunity to become better acquainted with prominent Japanese, to meet well-known American tourists promptly, and to work for the betterment of relations between our two countries. As the American Secretary, I tried hard to have the Japanese Army officers show some interest in that society but with absolutely no success. It was evident to me that all Japanese Army officers were afraid to have anything to do with that society. Even then the die was cast. The personnel of the Army no doubt felt that their next enemy would be America, and they did not want to be known among their brothers as pro-American. In this connection there was one time I had a grand opportunity to present my ideas on the America-Japan Society directly to the Minister of War and his staff officers. They were giving a luncheon for me before my return to my country. A number of prominent Americans were among the guests. I was slated for a speech. I took advantage of the situation to bring up the question of the society. A number of the usual hands across the sea speeches had been made by Japanese and Americans. Then, in my carefully prepared speech in Japanese, I brought out strongly but in rather a good natured way the fact that one of the best ways to immediately show their friendship would be for the Japanese Army officers to take more interest in that society. In fact I appealed directly and personally to the Minister of War to consider my suggestion favorably. I was not at all surprised by the reaction I got. They overwhelmed me with remarks about my fine talk and the remarkably correct pronunciation of Japanese but not one word from one of them on the subject of my talk. Yes, the die was cast even then. And I knew it as well as they.

The first official dinner that Gwynneth and I attended was at the big palace-like foreign-style house of Prince Tokugawa. Present were some members of the Tokugawa family, Colonel and Mrs. Burnett, and several leading American businessmen and their wives.

From then on we were gradually invited to dinner by all the various Ambassadors, Ministers, and Chargé d'Affaires, by all the Military Attachés, by many of the Secretaries of Staff, and Minister of War, and the Minister of the Navy. As a general rule, the wives were not included in the parties with the Army. They stuck closer to the old feudal customs than the other departments of the government. And I forgot to mention a very important host—the Minister of Foreign Affairs. His dinners were a special treat. His group, being traveled and accustomed to dealing with foreigners, knew better how to entertain them. Incidentally, their dinners were always unusual and especially good. I refer here to the selection of the food and its preparation. The Navy also was a much better host than the Army. Their visits to foreign ports had broadened them.

We had the privilege of enjoying many a fine party given primarily for our Ambassador or some distinguished tourists. I recall an outstanding affair given by the head of the celebrated Mitsui family at their foreign-style home used almost entirely I believe for the entertainment of foreigners. I think this particular party was for the Lindberghs when they visited Japan. The Mitsuis had several ways of entertaining us that evening, but I especially remember the second floor large hallway where a number of Japan's best artists were at work producing typical Japanese water colors. Before dinner we watched them working and after dinner, we were permitted to select one each and take it home with us. Gwynneth and I had ours later mounted on Kakemonos so we could hang them on our walls at home. Even today we prize them very much. The Mitsuis were very dignified and distant in their relations with foreigners. At least it seemed so to us. We never became really well acquainted with them.

Socially, our lives were very full—too full in fact. Not only were there the Japanese official group, the foreign diplomatic group, but there were also the Japanese business group, the American business group, both in Tokyo and in Yokohama, and then the prominent American tourists. Nearly every night we were either out to dinner or at home giving a dinner. Often one or both of us were out for luncheon. Many calls had to be made in the afternoons. Much of this life could not be considered a pleasure. We would like to have avoided much of it. Many a dinner or party we attended only because the position of the host made it mandatory. And many of the guests at our home were invited simply because they had previously entertained us. Many such an evening was spent in maneuvering to get the information from someone of those present who knew or were suspected to have certain facts I wished to know.

Entertainment was easy for us with our five to seven good servants. In fact, the servants always seemed pleased that we were going to have guests. Short notice did not discourage them. The wherewithals were always ready on time. They seemed to make a gay affair of a party. The cook's friends and several of the delivery boys would come in to help in the kitchen. We could hear them laughing and talking out in the kitchen during the period of preparation for the party, but after the guests began to arrive, the place would be absolutely quiet. They prepared excellent foreign food usually of the French or British style.

Some dishes were decidedly works of art. American tourists would marvel at them. Gwynneth gradually taught our cook many American dishes that were wanted especially by our children. Practically never did our children cause us any embarrassment before our guests. They were well disciplined in that way.

We had little work to do in connection with a dinner. Gwynneth prepared the list and sent out the invitations, prepared or at least checked the table decorations, approved the menu which the cook had drawn up, and prepared and placed the place cards on the table. For my part, I selected the wines and liqueurs and placed them in the pantry in the order in which they were to be served. Of course, if it were a stag affair, I would choose the guests and seat them. Usually the correct seating arrangement was not difficult to accomplish. Sometimes we had to ask the Embassy to decide for us. We never knew of anyone making a fuss over an incorrect seating except one of the Canadian Ministers. When a guest, the first thing he did after being seated was to check carefully to see that he had been placed in accordance with his rank. It was done very openly and twice as I recall we were present when he made it known he was not pleased with his seat. This was embarrassing to Gwynneth because often she found herself seated next to that Canadian Minister. In this connection, I want to mention that Gwynneth was almost always seated among much higher ranking people than I was because nearly always some of the top guests would be bachelors or widowers.

With reference to the use of alcoholic beverages, the flow of various kinds went about as follows, modified in accordance with the menu and the nationality of the guests: before dinner in the living room we served a cocktail, usually a dry Martini, with a big array of attractively prepared hors d'oeuvres. The Japanese servants were experts in making the accompaniment to a cocktail. At the table as soon as the soup was placed sherry was poured. Just before the fish course arrived Rhine or Moselle wine would be added; before the meat course, a Claret; and before the dessert, Port wine. If the entree course were chicken we probably would serve a Sauterne or other white wine. So you can see that your glassware constituted a large part of your table decoration—at least four wine glasses in addition to your water glass. Sometimes Burgundy and on special occasions Champagne. After dinner, the ladies withdrew to the living room while the men remained at the table or went to the library. Then, all were offered a small cup of strong coffee and the choice of several liqueurs. Of course the smoking supplies were then passed around. Smoking at the table was done but not encouraged by many hostesses because there had been too many expensive tablecloths ruined. Some hostesses when they knew the men were to remain at the table purposely did not use a fine tablecloth. Of course your cigars had to be good. I found it quite economical to have handy a box of Pittsburgh stogies. It aroused the curiosity of the Europeans who would insist on trying them, thus saving the price of an expensive cigar.

To wait on the table, to receive the guests at the door, and to see them out on their way home we hired two Japanese experts. They made a good appearance and handled everything in their line of duty skillfully.

Here I want to say something to the credit of our servants, and their many friends. Our liquors were kept in a special pantry that was never locked and yet I never missed a single bottle. Apparently, they never even took a drink from any bottle. And I never saw one of the house servants when he appeared to have been drinking. That was our experience and I suspect that it was not an unusual situation.

When we were entertaining Japanese only, we naturally brought out some good sake, the rice wine of Japan. That had to be a special brand, especially when the guests were Army and Navy officers. That special brand was not like the ordinary mild wine drunk by the Japanese. It was a very dry type with a superior taste, sort of a brandy.

With all that array of drinks, one might expect someone to get drunk but to the best of my memory, it did not happen in my home while I was in Japan.

It was quite noticeable that in the fall when the social season first opened, the guests would drink considerable wine and always take a liqueur. As the season wore on they would drink less and less until late in the spring the diplomats would hardly drink anything. I did not notice that let up in the American. He was always ready for a drink of good whiskey. Incidentally, when we were giving a dinner for Europeans we had to put forth our most expensive wines and liqueurs, but for a group of Americans we used poorer grades of wines while putting out our best in whiskey. Some of our British friends preferred to drink Scotch all evening without touching a cocktail, wine, or liqueur. Personally, I liked to do the same. I always felt better the next day when I touched nothing but whiskey.

One of our Ambassadors, "Governor" Forbes, imported his whiskey by the barrel from Ireland. It was the driest I have ever tasted with the softness of a lover's pat and the strength of the kick of a mule. One day he had me over to help him entertain the heads of missions of the Spanish-speaking countries. As they started to depart he quietly said to me, "Colonel, I have had a pitcher of that new whiskey of mine put on the table in the hall. Please see that each guest has the opportunity to sample it as he leaves." I obeyed efficiently and all guests left very happy, exclaiming what a wonderful host the American Ambassador was.

From my description of the use of liquor one might get the idea that a member of the diplomatic group would find it necessary to partake freely of alcoholic beverages. That is not so. During the tour of duty I had at the American Legation at Peking when a young Lieutenant I did not drink anything stronger than "Ginger Beer." When a young student officer at the Legation in Tokyo, I still did not take anything stronger than "Champagne Cider." In Peking the only group who made it difficult for me was the regimental officers at the British Legation Guard. One evening in Peking as I passed through the living room of the American Officers Mess someone of the older officers asked, "And where is our Lieutenant going this evening?" I replied, "To dinner at the German mess." Another officer then remarked, "Well, McIlroy, if you don't drink tonight you never will." Having had the experience with the Britishers I was a little uneasy but my fears were unnecessary. As soon as they noticed I was only touching my lips to the glass when toasts were offered, the officer who had asked me over said to me, "I see you are not drinking anything. Is there something you especially prefer?" I told him that I did not drink anything alcoholic. He immediately called a soldier and told him to take away all my drinks and to bring me soft drinks. Thereafter, I had no trouble whatever in that mess. But the time I went back to Japan as the Military Attaché I was drinking moderately, but there were both men and women in that diplomatic group who did not touch it. And I think they were not embarrassed in their abstinence. They either let the waiters fill their glasses and then did not touch it or they deliberately turned their glass over before the waiter arrived with each drink. I still find it less annoying to me to turn my coffee cup over at an evening dinner, for coffee still keeps me awake at nights. I hope this meets with the approval of Emily Post.

The food situation for us, both from the standpoint of the family and our formal dinners was much helped by the fact that we could order supplies in large quantities from the Army Commissary in Manila and received it by transport without the payment of any customs duty. This enabled our family to have daily many things to which they were accustomed in their own country and which could not be purchased in Japan. Also, it made it possible for our formal dinners to contain items on the menu that would be of special interest to other nationalities. One evening we gave a dinner for a group of Japanese General Staff Officers. Following the dinner, for their entertainment, I arranged on the mantel over the fireplace in our living room a row of items recently received from the Manila Commissary. Then we had the officers play various games of skill, such as trying to throw rings from one side of the room over a wooden upright peg at the other side of the room. The winner of each test had the privilege of selecting one item for a prize from the mantel. One of the first winners was Colonel Watari who had been a Military Attaché to Washington. He caused a loud laugh by passing up the more expensive articles and grabbing at once the cake of Ivory Soap.

During my stay in Japan as Military Attaché I had four different Chiefs of Mission. At first there was Mr. Neville of whom I have written before. In the spring of 1930 came Mr. Castle from Washington where I think he had been Undersecretary of State. He remained but a few months to carry out some special mission. Mr. Castle was a tall, dignified appearing gentleman who impressed everyone favorably. His wife caused quite a ripple of interest when they first arrived as she was one of the largest women physically I have ever seen. If there were a few critical remarks passed among the diplomatic group at first, in a short time one could hear nothing but praise of her. She was a brilliant woman, kind and thoughtful always toward others, no matter how low ranking you were. In spite of her physical handicap, she was the most punctilious of all the women of the diplomatic group in carrying out her social obligations.

After the return of the Castles to Washington, Mr. Neville again took the reins. He held them until early in 1931 when W. Cameron Forbes arrived.

It was while Mr. Castle was there that the cornerstone of the new American Embassy buildings was laid—May 30, 1930. An American Army Captain of the Corps of Engineers had been sent over with that difficult job of constructing a residence for our Ambassador, an office building for all American diplomatic officials, and several apartment buildings that would house a number of the staff. I kept in close touch with him. He certainly had a multitude of difficulties but by keeping on duty day and night and doing a lot of hard clever thinking he managed to accomplish what at times seemed almost impossible. He deserves great credit for that accomplishment.

His name is Thomas D. Stamps. He later became Professor of Engineering at West Point.

Mr. Forbes came from the elite group of Boston, a member of an old wealthy family, who added to his fortune and became a director in a number of important commercial companies of the United States. In spite of his active business connections he had already spent years in the service of his country in the Philippines. There he had been Governor for some time. Only recently I was talking to a retired Army officer who made the statement that Mr. Forbes had been the best Governor the Philippines ever had, and I can easily believe it. The same statement was made to me about a month ago by a former Secretary of Agriculture of the Philippines. Even when the "Governor" came to Japan he was still full of his experiences in those islands and liked best to talk about what ought to be done for the future of them. He seemed to have a difficult time transferring his intense interest to his new job. I think the fact that he was a bachelor handicapped him some socially. At first, he rented for his residence the home of Dr. Teussler, the head of the American St. Luke's Hospital. There, he had an attractive cousin come over to act as his hostess. Later, he moved into the newly constructed Ambassador's residence on the Embassy ground. There his hostess was a sister-in-law who came over with her daughter.

Before leaving this chapter, let me tell a story in connection with the Canadian Legation—a joke on me. Gwynneth and I were dressing for dinner at the Canadian Legation. I had laid out on my bed all that belonged to a formal dinner dress including the white tie and long tail coat. In the midst of our dressing a phone call came from the Canadian Legation suggesting that their guests wear black tie and tuxedo coat. Hurriedly, I jerked off my white tie and white waistcoat and redressed more informally as requested. When we arrived at the Legation we were soon informed that the reason for the change in dress was their late decision to take their guests after dinner to the amateur theatrical at the Imperial Hotel assembly room. Imagine my surprise when after removing my hat and coat and looking into the long mirror in the men's room, I beheld myself still in a long tailed coat. In my haste at home in making the change, I had picked up the wrong coat. This was a serious matter for me. There I was with a low collar, black tie, black waistcoat and over it all a formal long tailed coat. Such an outfit just is not worn. I looked ridiculous. What to do? I asked one of the servants to call my chauffeur. We met at the front door. He was sent flying to our home to bring the tuxedo. Then I had to go in and speak to the host and hostess and guests and explain my irregular costume and my hopes for correcting it. There was much laughter at my expense, in fact, the incident made the party a success from the very start. Shortly after we had been seated at dinner, word came that the important coat had arrived so I excused myself and soon returned in proper habiliments. No doubt that story went the rounds of the diplomatic group.

So after dinner we went on, properly attired, to the amateur theatrical. A series of plays were put on every year, some of them by a group in Yokohama and some by a group in Tokyo. The audience at the Imperial Hotel theater was unique. Usually the boxes were occupied by the Ambassadors and Ministers and their families. The audience was largely composed of Europeans and Americans with a sprinkling of Japanese and South Americans. During the intervals between acts, we would go about conversing with our friends in the boxes and elsewhere. It was imperative that we say good evening to all the chiefs of mission present. We knew almost everyone present in the audience. The acting was often very good. "Governor" Forbes took a personal interest in the amateur plays when he was our Ambassador, and it was quite evident that he knew his stuff.

During my tour in Japan both as a student and when Military Attaché, I often felt the need of some written guide that one could consult for information as to what was expected of us under various circumstances both officially and socially. When on duty in my own country I had formed the habit of leaving my successor a written account of my duties, the troubles one encountered, and how to avoid them. It seems to me that some such papers should be required of every government official before he turns his job over to another. Such a custom would be of great help in Tokyo, for sometime as Military Attaché I decided to write up, not regulations exactly, but a guide to help my subordinates know what was expected of them both officially and socially in Japan. When I made my intentions known to my chief, Mr. Neville, he laughed and said he would not advise it. He remarked something about the less you put in writing the less apt you are to get into trouble. I replied that I had been trained to take responsibility and that when I made a mistake I was not afraid to acknowledge it. Is it not possible that the training of our diplomats in those days lacked something? It always seemed so to me. It is hoped that while General Marshall was Secretary of State he took the opportunity to change some of that attitude. Mr. Neville did not approve my idea but did not forbid it, so before long that guide came into existence and was issued to my subordinates. I hope it has been of use to succeeding groups going to Japan. Of course such a guide would soon become obsolete in details unless revamped from time to time by each Military Attaché.

Also, I started another custom of keeping sort of an official diary. After each official function or party I attended, I wrote up an account of everything connected with it that might be of interest to the next Military Attaché to read before he attended such an affair. One copy I kept and the other was placed in the files of the office. Later in this book I will quote from that diary.

One year the British Embassy invited us to a big fancy dress party. Gwynneth and I blew ourselves for old fashioned Japanese costumes. We bought them from a store that supplied the Japanese actors. Mine was the dress of a high ranking Daimyo of the feudal days—a complete outfit including shoes, underwear, wig, and two imitation swords. Gwynneth's was a gorgeous old fashioned set of long-tailing kimonos but she just could not stand for the wig, so heavy and awful looking to foreigners. We still have those unusual costumes but we have never had the nerve to appear in them in this country. Someone tell us what to do with them.

Writing about costumes reminds me to discuss the clothing necessary at that time for an officer on such duty. It was amazing the quantity and variety needed on that assignment. A list of them might be of interest in these days of more simple dressing.

Uniforms:

Military full dress with much gold, with both trousers and breeches, and black boots
Social evening military full dress
Overcoat, woolen
Raincoat

Blue Dress uniform
White Dress uniform
White mess jacket with black trousers
Olive drab field uniform, wool, with tan leather
boots, trousers, and breeches

Civilian clothing:

Full dress long evening coat and trousers
Tuxedo coat
Long morning coat and trousers
Short morning coat and trousers
Several winter business suits
Summer pongee silk suits, six or more
Tennis trousers, wool and cotton ones
Overcoat, dark blue
Overcoat, brown

The above together with all the various shirts, ties, shoes, etc., made a complicated mess. All the above clothing I brought back to this country but there has been little use for most of it outside the business suits. Gradually it has been disappearing to the Salvation Army.

My clothing problem was bad enough but think of Gwynneth with herself and five children to keep clothed properly. And in Japan it was very difficult at that time to find presentable clothing for foreign women and children.

Photo Section Captions

Page 94   J.G. McIlroy—1918, age 37.

Page 95   Col. McIlroy with son, Garfield, and daughter, Katharine, enroute to diplomatic event, Tokyo, Japan, 1932.

Page 96   Lt. Col. J.G. McIlroy, at Fort Benjamin Harrison, Indiana, just prior to receiving orders for Japan as U.S. Military Attaché, 1928, age 48.

Page 97   Unveiling of memorial to U.S. General Grant in Tokyo, 1931. Left to right: Baron Matsuda, Jane Susan, and Viscount Shibusawa.

Page 98   Guam Governor Commander Bradley and family visiting Col. McIlroy's family in Tokyo, (c. 1930).

Page 99   Private luncheon for Charles and Anne Lindbergh, Tokyo, 1931 (Charles in back, second from left—Anne seated, far right). Photo taken by Lt. Col. McIlroy.

Page 100   Newly commissioned 3rd Officer WAAC, Jane McIlroy, Ft. Des Moines, Iowa, 1942, age 22.

Page 101   1st Lt. WAC-AC, Jane McIlroy, McChord Field, Washington, 1945, age 25. Jane was a public relations officer and base historian.

Page 102   1st Lt. Jane McIlroy, McChord Field, Washington (last picture taken in uniform at the end of World War II).

Page 103   Col. J.G. McIlroy, U.S. Army Retired, 1946.

Page 104   (top) Lt. Col. J.G. McIlroy, Jr., F-15 pilot, lost in flight over Korea, 1954, age 39.

              (bottom) Col. J.G. McIlroy, U.S. Army Retired (last picture taken), age 75.

94

464 BUI9 OCT44 (IO83) AIR MEDAL PRESENTATION Mᶜ CFW

XII

Family Life

Our family life in Japan was very pleasant—what there was of it. If we were home and not entertaining we had plenty of time to be with the children as practically all work in and out of the house was well handled by the servants. We seldom had dinner with them except on Sunday. If we were going out for dinner, they would have their dinner before the time for us to depart so then we could visit with them. During the week days of the school term they were absent at lunch for they all attended the American School in Japan. But we always breakfasted together. When possible, they were driven to and from school by our chauffeur but much of the time they had to take the Japanese street cars.

Much of the satisfaction in living in Japan came from our excellent servants. The first group, which we took over from the Burnetts, did not work out well. None of them did their jobs well. Their loyalty appeared to be still with the Burnetts and their way of doing things. We finally had to let them go. Then we secured a well-recommended young cook, a young man who had been raised on a farm. He largely selected the other servants for us. They became a part of the family almost, efficient and loyal, always on the job. And they were like a happy family among themselves. One nurse maid we had during an earthquake would always shield the body of our baby with her own body and never think of phoning her own family to learn how they were until the excitement was all over in our family.

When our baby daughter arrived in March 1931, family life was more interesting for us all. Incidentally, Japan was a great place for American women to have their children. It seemed to us that every wife of an American in Japan had either just had a child or was about to have one. That was the main topic of conversation when American woman came together. You see in Tokyo there was the American St. Luke's Hospital run by that able Dr. Teussler. That hospital had splendid Japanese doctors and nurses, some of the best in Japan and that is saying a good deal. And after the mother returned home from the hospital with her child the care of the baby was so easy because of the excellent and loyal baby nurses. All our servants in fact used to clamor for the privilege of looking after our youngest. The cook insisted on his right to have her for an half hour just after breakfast.

But the family situation was not serene at all times. For instance, one day I received a telephone call from the American superintendent of the American School in Japan about my ten-year-old daughter. He said that she had struck the son of the Mexican Ambassador, that he had suspended her, and that she would not be permitted back at school until I came out and straightened things out. The call peeved me, especially the suspension. But I went out at once. My daughter claimed that the boy was pestering her and preventing her from doing her work. He did not heed her warning so she struck him. The boy was able bodied and old enough to look out for himself. However, I do suspect that the blow was one to remember for that daughter was very strong, a fine physical specimen. I told my daughter that she should learn how to handle the boys in a less crude manner, but I told the superintendent that I thought he had made too much of the affair and that he should have handled it himself. As bad luck would have it, Gwynneth and I had our first invitation to dinner at the Mexican Embassy that very evening. We went along with considerable uneasiness as to what our reception would be like. To our surprise, we were treated with unusual courtesy and really enjoyed the evening very much.

In fairness to this daughter it would now seem to be the time to tell about the affair in which she took a prominent part to the credit of the family. I refer to the ceremony of the unveiling of the Grant Memorial in Ueno Park, in Tokyo. The moving spirit back of this memorial was the venerable and distinguished Japanese man of big business, Baron Shibusawa. Our chargé d'affaires called me in and told me that my ten-year-old daughter had been chosen for the honor of unveiling the memorial. This because my father had served under General Grant in the Civil War. Gwynneth and I were at once concerned over the possible effect this publicity would have on Jane Susan. We decided that it would be advisable to tell her nothing about her being expected to take any part in the ceremony for fear it might upset her nervously. During the ceremony our family sat in the front row of seats, with my ten-year-old at my side. The program ran off beautifully and when they tipped me that it was time for us to perform I turned to her and said, "Jane, we are going up on the stage. You come with me and do what I tell you to do." She did not have time to become embarrassed.

On the stage, I placed the ropes in her hands and told her to hold them until I told her otherwise. She looked very sweet and pretty—unembarrassed—just interested.

Soon we told her to pull. She did, and out came the very nice memorial to General Grant. Pictures of the event appeared in the Japanese and American papers. Many people asked us how we had managed to have Jane do her part so nicely. In this connection, I should say that General Grant's popularity with the Japanese came from his visit to that country after he had ceased to be President of the United States. The Japanese had appreciated his very evident deep interest in their country and its people. One of his acts, which especially endeared him to them, occurred in the beautiful setting of Nikko. Here, there is a rushing mountain stream that must be crossed in order to visit the ornate Buddhist temples in their beautiful hillside setting among the tall cryptemerias. There were then two bridges over the stream. The one for the people is an unpainted, dull gray structure but the other is painted a brilliant red with its general appearance similar to that of the temples. It has always been reserved for the Emperor only. It seems that the Japanese offered it to General Grant as a special privilege and that he tactfully declined to cross it, using instead the bridge used by all the people.

Another thing that upset the even tenor of family life frequently was the earthquakes. Hardly a day went by without a tremor of some kind. At times, they were quite strong, strong enough to frighten us and cause us to run out into the garden or take other precautions such as getting in a doorway. Unfortunately, they seemed to have a preference for the middle of the night after we were all in bed and asleep. To be awakened rudely from your sleep did not tend to give you a quiet set of nerves to start off with. You were scared before you got your mind working properly.

Sometimes the earthquakes would come in groups.

In the winter of 1931-1932 we had a series of strong earthquakes lasting for over a month. Our youngest daughter was a baby then. Her bedroom adjoined ours on the second floor. Before retiring, Gwynneth and I would place some clothes handy to draw on quickly in case we were awakened by a severe quake in the night. Time after time for weeks that winter we were awakened rudely by Mother Earth. It always alarmed us. I usually walked over and sat in one of the bedroom windows—on the sill. Sometime I would become sufficiently alarmed to hustle downstairs and outside. But Gwynneth never hesitated. She would slip on her kimono and slippers, rush to the baby in her crib, hurry downstairs with her and out into the garden. At the foot of the stairs she would always be met by the nurse who slept on the first floor. As a rule the older children slept through the quakes and I thought it best not to awaken them. Just took the chance.

While we were in Japan we were fortunate that no really serious earthquake took place where we were. Upon arriving in Japan, the average person treats the first weak ones he notices with amusement, but after experiencing one of the stronger ones, he will consider them a joke no longer. It peeves the older residents to hear tourists saying how much they hope there will be an earthquake before they leave Japan. Quite often the tourist is more than satisfied before he departs.

My predecessor, Colonel Burnett, had been there during the terrible earthquake of September 1923. Their home burned with all their lovely Japanese art treasures. Yokohama was totally destroyed and 100,000 people lost their lives. At that time, I was in charge of Japanese Intelligence in Washington. I recall placing a large map of the situation on an easel in the office of the Secretary of War and keeping all information received on it for over a week. Several times the Secretary and I, with the map, called on the President. The awful details of that disaster and the terrible pictures I received of it were strongly engraved on my memory, all of which did not tend to cause me to take a quake in Japan with indifference.

During the summers the family enjoyed life at Karuizawa, the resort in the mountains to the west of Tokyo. There were swimming, bicycling, tennis, walking in the hills, and the ever interesting volcano, Asama, for us all to watch. In the late summer there was a tennis tournament in which nearly everyone took part either as a player or an interested onlooker. There were many beautiful views to repay one for a long hike up one of the many high hills just at sunset. Horses were available for those who enjoyed riding through the mountains. Asama San was so interesting because it was so inconsistent and irregular in its moods. It was decidedly active much of the time, sometimes throwing up big hot rocks, sometimes throwing forth ashes drifting down, often puffing out huge billows of black smoke, and at long intervals lava would overflow.

There was plenty of informal social life there also. In the village there were Japanese tradesmen largely, but in the hills about, the cottages were occupied largely by foreigners—missionaries, businessmen, diplomats, and their families.

Usually I went up on Friday afternoon by train. Sometimes I spent more than a weekend. This was when there was work that could be taken with me and accomplished just as well at a desk away from my office. At Takasaki, where the train stopped long enough to take on its mountain engine, there was something to which I always looked forward. One of the food sales boys kept a few quart bottles of good beer on ice in a box on the station platform for the few foreigners who would appreciate it. That beer went nicely with a layer of hot eels on hot rice in a clean little pine box making a light supper fit for a king.

In the fall of 1931 we were lucky enough to be able to rent a better house for less money. It was on a hill near Shinagawa Station in the south of Tokyo toward Yokohama. It had been owned by a wealthy Japanese who lost his money. The renting of that house was so easy that I always suspected that the Japanese Army Intelligence group might have had a hand in it. In other words, I suspected it might be wired to listen to our conversations, but I never could locate any wires. The front of the house was a large foreign-style structure with a library and two living rooms on the first floor and four bedrooms on the second floor. In the rear was a well-built Japanese-style addition with three rooms on the first floor and two rooms on the second floor. The library I took as my office, the office force was placed in the large living room and we used the other living room for its true purpose. The children took over the foreign-style bedrooms. In the Japanese part we opened up the rooms on the first floor as one big dining room, while Gwynneth and I took over the large beautiful bedroom on the second floor and placed our baby in the small one adjoining. I recall the ceiling of our bedroom was made of a beautifully grained knotty pine, the boards all coming from the same trunk for the same array of knots ran all the way across the room. Of course, in accordance with Japanese custom, this wood was untreated. Many a morning I lay there just before rising examining the beautiful grain designs in that ceiling.

At the side of the house was a large Japanese garden with flowers always blooming, and in the rear was a tennis court, which was made good use of by the family. On the debit side of that house there was the trouble we had with the cess pool. It was not constructed for a family of our size and an office force in addition. In the rear of the Japanese addition were two Japanese toilets. And did we know when the "Honey Man" paid us a visit!!!

In the garden was a large aviary, the usual gold fish pool, the red leafed maples, a large wisteria arbor, a concrete terrace lined with azalea, artistic stepping stones here and there, and throughout the middle a nice green lawn.

The Japanese family life was an interesting study for Gwynneth and me. It was impossible to actually see what went on in the high class families secluded as they were by their high walls or bamboo fences, but the life in the lower class families appeared to be largely open to the public. So many of the poorer families, especially those of the owners of the small shops, had their homes right on the street. Many an evening after dinner Gwynneth and I walked through those narrow streets observing the family scenes. The front of the small shop or home, usually the same, would be open during most of the year. Often the family would be in the room next to the street sitting about on their cushions on the floor, or in the winter circled about the big fire box in the center of the room, reading, conversing, or playing, all under the one electric light bulb suspended by its cord from the center of the ceiling.

These family pictures were never ending source of interest and amusement to us. Nearly always it was a happy group we saw, a group in which the children were the more important. The adoration of the parents for those children was so very evident. Often I caught a part of their conversation which helped us much in understanding them. Most of what we saw on these nightly strolls was a decided credit to the Japanese people. (During a social studies class cleaning the basement of an

American School building, an American flag was found by this same Mexican boy. He immediately taunted the ten-year-old McIlroy daughter by stomping the flag into the pathway cinders. She hauled off with another fist to his chest, and rescued the flag. Chastised by the principal at the time, he later called her to his office and presented to her the laundered flag for her to have! She hung it over her bed, longing to be back in the good old USA!)

XIII
Imperial Parties

Throughout the year a number of unusual parties were given by the Imperial Household Department. Among these were the Spring Ch Garden Party, the Fall Chrysanthemum Garden Party, the Duck Hunt, the Fishing Party, and the Imperial Reception or Audience at New Year's. The guests at these parties included high ranking government officials and foreign diplomats. Sometimes a few prominent foreign tourists were included upon the recommendations of the various ambassadors.

I know that obligation of asking the Japanese Government to invite American tourists by name to those Imperial Parties was a very difficult problem for our Embassy. Not all tourists were a credit to our country. And of course, the type we would hope would not ask to go were the very ones most insistent that an invitation be obtained for them. They were the type who would take much of our time telling about their unpleasant experiences with the Japanese police and plainclothesmen. Often they had just come from visiting China where they had been able to be just as domineering as they wished over the native. Coming to Japan they seemed to resent not being able to treat the Japanese in the same way. And of course the Japanese police went out of their way often to show those people that they were in a different country from China.

114

When that type of tourist did get to a party I have often heard their women talking loudly making fun of their hosts—this when they were standing among Japanese people who probably spoke better English than they did. The Japanese never said anything in reply, but I have thought that many of those uncomplimentary remarks were stored up in the minds of those Japanese officials and that this might account sometimes for their cruel treatment of American prisoners during World War II.

At the Garden Parties, the guests upon arrival were expected to spend some time strolling about the big beautiful garden viewing the many trees, shrubs, and flowers. Those gardens were indeed worth looking over. They made me think of a fairyland. There I saw my first chrysanthemum plants with hundreds of blossoms on a single plant. As we strolled about, we stopped now and then to chat with Japanese or foreign acquaintances. Later we would be assembled to bow to the Imperial Family upon their arrival.

This was followed by the heads of the various Missions introducing their newly arrived members to the Emperor, the Empress, or both as the occasion required. There comes back to me my first experience in Japan of that kind. I was being presented to the old Emperor Meiji by our then Minister, Thomas J. O'Brien, a grand and able man. But he made the mistake of introducing me as Lieutenant George V. Strong, who lived with me when we were student officers at the Legation. He immediately corrected himself but the Emperor and I had a laugh at his expense.

During my four years as the Military Attaché I met the present Emperor many times. Upon arrival and departure I was granted an audience at which time we exchanged a few carefully prepared sentences in the presence of a household official and the American Chief of Mission. Also, I was presented at the yearly Army maneuvers. This was done right in the field in front of the Emperor's private tent. At those maneuvers he appeared as the Commanding Officer of all those troops and certainly conducted himself as such.

To get back to the Garden Parties, the reception being over, there would be a tea or light lunch served at tables in the open. The foreign women were always much interested in watching the women of the Imperial Family in their brave effort to handle themselves in the foreign manner. They would be wearing foreign-style clothing, which would look odd on them. I always thought they made a mistake in not sticking to their own beautiful kimonos in which they looked so well. After the Imperial luncheon or tea, the Imperial Family would withdraw while the guests all bowed low. Those Imperial gardens were well worth seeing, in fact, real works of art.

The Duck Hunt was decidedly an unusual experience. Nothing like what one would expect of a Duck Hunt. A comparatively small group of the diplomats was invited for any particular party. The one I attended had as guests largely Americans and just a few others who might fit in well. We went out to the duck lake in a special interurban street car which easily held all our party. That year the Crown Prince Chichibu and his Princess were our host and hostess.

Soon after boarding the car I found myself seated beside the Princess, enjoying a conversation about Washington, D.C., where she had been partly educated during her father's tour there as the Ambassador from Japan. My pleasure, however, was short-lived for soon the American Ambassador, W. Cameron Forbes, came over, seated himself on the other side and engaged her immediately in conversation. Quite evidently it was my move and move I did to some less desirable location. You have probably sensed that the Princess was attractive. Well, she was and she talked good American, too. And it was very evident that she liked to talk to Americans. Miniature golf was one of the new games at that time. Our Ambassador invited me to join the Prince and him in a game. While we were playing, the Prince took out a cigarette whereupon I proudly jerked out my new efficient lighter given me by a visiting American air pilot. The Prince showed much interest in that lighter so I told him to just keep it. About two months later, I saw copies of that lighter in the market marked "Made in Japan."

In the building was a place where one could be served with little tidbits of duck meat, which they cooked for you over a little copper and wood fire box. It made such a hit that we asked the Japanese in charge to have one made for us. He said he could do that. So two months later, it came along. Later, when back in this country, we had it copied so that we could have two to help out in our giving of Japanese-style dinners. At noon a good foreign-style lunch was served us.

During the day we were divided into groups of about eight for the hunting. Not far away from the club building was a lake of about twenty acres. It was full of wild ducks attracted there by the good food put out. From the side of the lake next to the club building there were little canals, about three feet wide and four feet deep extending out for about eighty feet from the lake. At the near end of each canal was a blind behind which each group hastily assembled after being called up for the next try. There the attendant organized us in two lines of four each. In those canals had been placed food to attract the ducks. The attendant watched the canal through a slit in the blind.

117

Each of us was here given an imposing weapon consisting of a long light pole on the end of which was attached a two foot ring of iron to which was fastened a net. When the attendant saw ducks in the canal he signaled us and we ran around four to each side of the canal. When the ducks heard us they would fly up out of the canal and it was up to us to catch one in the net as it tried to escape. For the average man with any athletic training, it was a cinch. When you caught one you threw your net well to the rear where one of the attendants would remove the duck and quickly kill it by twisting its head under a wing. As soon as your duck was out of the net, you were free to try to catch another but usually no second effort was successful, for generally, the ducks would have escaped by that time. The women took part in this sport (?) as well as the men. Most of them seemed to enjoy it.

When it came time to go home you might think that each family would receive the number of ducks they had caught. Not at all. It went by rank. The Ambassador received the most, the Counselor next, then the Military Attaché and so on down the line. But we received enough for our purposes, enough to have a good meal for both ourselves and our servants.

The Fishing Party took place in a relatively small park garden between Shimbashi Station and Tokyo Bay. I suppose there were not over ten acres in the grounds, much of which was occupied by a large pond. The guests, each time, apparently consisted of about half of the diplomatic group. At least the upper half in rank of about half of the countries represented in Tokyo. That which I recall most clearly is the incident I will now try to describe to you.

As I walked into the grounds I saw a lot of men of a variety of nationalities in frock coats and silk hats standing at varying intervals along the bank of the pond fishing very intently. But they were not all men for soon I noticed a fisherwoman half hidden by the shrubbery—a huge foreign European woman. I stopped to observe her fishing technique. While standing there I noticed coming toward me the lovely Belgian Countess, wife of the Belgian Counselor and daughter of the Belgian Ambassador, who was Dean of the Diplomatic Corps at that time. She was dressed in a new striking Paris creation, light blue in color, with a magnificent large beautiful hat. She was the picture of loveliness, happiness, and with a smile that would win anyone. As she approached I started to put forth my best greeting, raising my silk hat, but just then I became conscious that the fisherwoman had hooked a good-sized fish which she had pulled from the water with a powerful effort and was swinging over her head well to her rear. To my amazement, the fish splashed with a resounding thud right against the breast of the beautiful Countess. That was a catastrophe. I have never seen such a sudden complete change come over the face of anyone as took place on the face of the recipient on this occasion. That lovely expression of the moment before changed to the most vindictive picture of ugly hate one could ever see. And that gorgeous hat had been jarred off its base so that it had anything but a dignified appearance. My own feelings were a mixture of disgust at the carelessness of the dowager fisherwoman, dismay at what had happened, and a strong desire to laugh long and loud. I think the Countess must have seen some of the latter, for dabbing at her front frantically with her lace handkerchief, she turned quickly away not waiting for me to finish my salutation and express my sympathy. She was not seen again at that party. The fisherwoman I suspect never did know the havoc she had wrought.

Every spring there was an Imperial Review at the Yoyogi Parade Grounds in the western edge of Tokyo. The Emperor himself, like a commanding officer, reviewed those troops collected from posts near Tokyo. On such occasions the foreign Military Attachés were mounted and accompanied the Emperor on his inspection of the troops and were placed near him as he took the salutes of the troops passing in review. At such a time, I was dressed in my very best including light blue breeches with a wide white stripe and tall black boots. Some foreigners were permitted to attend. One year we dressed up my son and one daughter and took them along. For such reviews the Emperor always appeared in his full-dress Army uniform mounted on his white Arabian steed. In all it must have been quite a physical ordeal for him to go through. At such times it was very noticeable that all our horses were very quiet and dependable. None of them became excited over anything, even if the band should start with a bang real close to us. They must have been selected and trained with great care.

Every fall Army maneuvers on a large scale were held in some part of Japan. Several divisions would be concentrated for this purpose. It was the culmination of months of maneuvers beginning with company training late in the summer. These maneuvers gave their officers much valuable training. They lasted three days during all of which the Emperor would be present. He would be taken to the maneuver section of the country in his special train, billeted near the opposing Armies, and every morning taken out to a position on some hill from which he would be able to observe most of the anticipated action for that day. We Military Attachés would be on another hill nearby. Always present was that white horse on which he would ride from his train or motor car to the hill and after the day's fight was over would again mount and ride back to his transportation.

At the close of the third day of mock fighting the mass of troops in the two opposing Armies would be arranged in two lines about fifteen feet apart facing each other and then the Emperor on his white horse would ride between the two long lines looking them over. This was one of the many ways they had of convincing the soldier that their Emperor was their real Commanding Officer and as such he had a great personal interest in them.

During those three days of maneuvering we Military Attachés had an interesting time. Each day we spent hours watching the battle but our Japanese General Staff guides always found time to take us to some nearby places of note for sight-seeing. The local Governor and Mayor usually presented us with some remembrance of the occasion. For instance, I note now on my desk a good silver cigarette case given us the year the maneuvers were in the Osaka area. Engraved on the cover is a drawing of the Osaka Castle. Inside are the signatures of the Governor and Mayor.

The Japanese people would come from considerable distance to line up along the fields to watch the maneuvers all day long. No doubt they had the hope that they might catch a glimpse of their god-like Emperor. My experience in observing that extreme veneration with which he was held by his subjects might be interesting. One afternoon, late after the troop movements for the day were over, I managed to lose our guides and was walking by myself toward our place of rendezvous. I found myself in a small village in the open square adjoining the railway station. This open space about the station was filled with Japanese men, women, and children. They were packed in, most of them sitting on straw mats placed on the ground. Evidently, they had been there a long time hoping to see the Emperor's train as it passed through. Fortunately, for me, as I stood there studying that large group the Imperial Train did move slowly into sight and then stopped between us and the setting sun.

We had read and been told so much about how the Japanese people worshipped their Emperor, so with that large group of Japanese of both sexes and of all ages before me I realized that it would be a good opportunity to observe their true reactions in the presence of their Emperor—at a time when they were not aware that they were being observed by a foreigner. Most of the people were no longer sitting but had changed to their knees with their heads bowed very low. You know the strict rule of conduct in the presence of the Emperor required a Japanese to bow his head and not to look upon him. To my amusement I noted that nearly all of them took brief stolen glances at the train now and then. Then I witnessed an unusual thing. I definitely saw the Emperor walking slowly through the car which was visible to most of the group. I will never forget the very audible and strange sound that came to me from that group before me, as they suddenly realized that they had seen their god in person right before them. It was probably a low intake of breath which they unconsciously did as their stolen glance took in the unusual situation. To me, it was overwhelming proof of the veneration in which the Japanese were said to hold their ruler. There was no possible doubt about the great thrill that group received from seeing their religious head in that car outlined against the setting sun.

The day following the end of the maneuvers was a busy one for us Military Attachés. First came the Imperial Review of all troops taking part in the maneuvers. This was followed by an imperial luncheon for all officers of those troops, and later for us the preparation for departure and the actual getting under way for our return to Tokyo.

Of course at the end of the maneuvers the uniforms of the Japanese soldiers would be in bad condition. In the first place, for all field work the Japanese soldier habitually wore old and much patched uniforms. But at the reviews they always appeared in fresh, clean uniforms, both officers and soldiers, so undoubtedly, they had shipped to them an extra good uniform.

At such reviews the Military Attachés were present at the reviewing position with the Emperor's staff. I was impressed by the tattered old colors carried by the troops. Usually they consisted of nothing but the faded colorless fringe of the original silk colors received upon the formation of the regiment many years ago. We were told that a regiment seldom received a second colors and that they only carried national colors—no regimental colors.

Those Japanese troops were not supplied and equipped with the latest and best of arms and transportation, far from it. They showed the result of the many recent years during which the liberal peace loving group of Japanese officials had given little money for the upkeep of their Army. But they did impress one with the idea that they were a hardy, well-disciplined, highly trained force which through determined aggressive action would get the most possible out of the equipment they had.

In my reports, I insisted that a regiment of well-trained American troops could defeat a regiment of Japanese troops. But on the other hand, I warned our War Department that in case of war with Japan we could expect to be at the receiving end for some time because they would have a large well-trained Army, and we would have comparatively an untrained mob with which to try to stop them. Our few trained soldiers would have to be used as instructors. I also claimed that Japan could take the Philippines whenever she decided to do it. I fear that the expression of these and similar opinions tended to give me a reputation in the War Department of being pro-Japanese.

A grand luncheon followed closely after the review. In a pleasant setting there would be about two acres hidden by a high fence made of immense bolts of cloth of the Japanese national colors, white and red. Inside at one end of the inclosure would be a large raised platform under a large tent. There on that platform the Emperor and a few guests of importance and rank would eat. Running perpendicular to that end of the field were many wooden tables covered with all sorts of good cold foreign-style foods and drinks. The Military Attachés were assigned a table near the Emperor's tent. The Japanese officers present seem to have no assigned tables but no doubt they came in as units and took tables as units. All stood except those on the Emperor's platform.

During the meal a number of officers were called to the platform if not already there, to receive special decorations. There was absolutely no hilarity of any kind. All guests remained very quiet, even talking in low tones. Before we left we were each given an attractively wrapped box of Japanese food, a gift from the Emperor. By custom, a gift was not opened in the presence of the giver. I always took mine home to the servants, who appeared to be very pleased to have them. We found the food in those boxes very interesting to look at—not to eat.

The Imperial New Year's Reception

This was the affair looked forward to so much by the ladies of the diplomatic corps. It meant to them beautiful new gowns with those long trailing trains. The men might be interested in seeing the first one of these shows but after that it appeared to be only a useless expenditure of money for those trains.

During the years I was a student, 1908–1911, we all went in carriages. But while I was the Military Attaché, 1929–1933, motor cars had taken the place of the carriages. As we approached the outer gate of the palace grounds it seemed that everyone was arriving at the same time. Motor cars were arriving from all directions. Naturally everyone tried to arrive at the exact time stated. We chased across the two bridges and through the ancient oriental gates in a steady stream of vehicles. Since only one car at a time could enter the "porte cochere" (as we U.S.'ers call it), there was soon formed a long column of panting cars waiting to discharge their gorgeous contents.

We dismounted at the entrance to the large one-storied Japanese-style sprawling building, which is near the Emperor's residence. We disposed of our outer wraps and signed a guest book after which we were directed through a long winding corridor to a very large waiting room, which soon filled up with all the members of the Diplomatic Corps in Tokyo.

It was a brilliant sight with the men generally in gorgeous uniforms and the ladies in their very, very, best with the long trains and some even with the tall feathers in their hair. My uniform consisted of a double-breasted dark blue frock coat with a double row of gold buttons down the front, and gold epaulets or rather knots on the shoulders. My trousers were a light blue with a wide white stripe. On my left shoulder (or was it the right) a long gold aiguillette, which designated a Military Aide status. In this case I was supposed to be the Aide of the Ambassador. Anyway, it helped out the uniform. Enroute I wore a blue cloth cap with a black gold-encrusted patent leather visor and with two narrow gold bands and one wide light blue band around it. But the most impressive thing of all was that long full circle cape of heavy dark blue broadcloth, with a lining of light blue cloth denoting Infantry, and a collar of black velvet. But even then I was thrown in the shade by the British Military Attaché with his very colorful and striking Highland costume. It was just out of this world.

The American diplomats wore formal civilian evening clothes, that is the long-tailed coat with white waistcoat and white tie. But the civilians of other nations had special diplomatic uniforms with much gold braid and many decorations. It seemed to me that the magnificence of the uniforms of the civilian diplomats went inversely as the importance of their country.

In that waiting room, we lingered about forty-five minutes. It gave all the opportunity to meet each other and look over all the wearing apparel. Finally, the hour arrived and we were conducted through some more corridors to the throne room. We moved in one long column, Ambassadors first according to their rank, each followed by his own embassy personnel according to rank of our departments. For instance, following our Ambassador and his wife went the Counselor and his wife, followed again by the other members of our State Department Foreign Service according to rank, each accompanied by his wife, if any. After the State Department came the Army personnel according to rank, then the Navy and at the rear the members of the Commerce Department. The countries with Ministers followed those with Ambassadors. Rank between Ambassadors and Ministers was determined by the length of time they had been on duty in Tokyo.

As we approached the entrance to the throne room we could look into the large room, see to the left side the throne of the Emperor with him seated thereon, at his left, the Empress on her throne and at her left, a charming group of Princesses standing.

Each person entered the throne room alone at the signal of the official of the Household Department, husbands first, each followed by his wife, if any.

The women had practiced for weeks to make sure that they could handle themselves correctly during that important minute or two. The men too probably practiced a little when no one was looking. We men were most emphatically cautioned about not withdrawing too rapidly after bowing to the Empress for we might step on the train of the lady ahead of us, causing a major catastrophe. Usually, there were uniformed pages at hand to assist with the trains if it became necessary. Let me tell you of the bad scare my Ambassador's wife gave me once when I was a student there. Our group had arrived at the door of the throne room. It was a small group in those days. In fact, it was only a Legation. So we were clustered as it were near our Minister and Mrs. O'Brien, who were then waiting for the signal to enter. Mrs. O'Brien had requested pages to handle her train and she was worried because there were no pages in sight. She turned to me and asked if I would be good enough to look after her train as she went in. Most reluctantly I promised to do so knowing well what a ribbing would be coming my way later from my confreres. The signal came, Mr. O'Brien went in,

Mrs. O'Brien prepared for her start and I made ready to command the train. But suddenly, two pages jumped out of hiding and I gladly retired to my place in ranks.

But to come back to our experience when I was the Military Attaché. I entered the throne room about twenty feet in rear of the last person connected with our Foreign Service. Advancing with dignity a few steps I stopped and bowed low from the hips while facing the Emperor. Taking a few more deliberate steps I bowed again to the Emperor. Then I moved forward till I was at attention fifteen feet in front of the Emperor. Again, I bowed low. Moving sideways about three yards I came to attention in front of the Empress and bowed low to her. Then I proceeded to back slowly out to the right rear making sure that I did not rush the lady in my rear and at the same time doing all I could to look over the Princesses as they stood there in foreign gowns. It appeared to me that those Japanese women were really getting quite a kick out of watching the foreigners go through that performance. I have detected their starting to laugh when something unusual happened in front of them but they always quickly regained control of themselves.

Gwynneth followed me going directly to a position in front of Emperor where she curtseyed with her right knee to the floor. Moving to her own right to a position in front of the Empress she curtseyed again after which she backed to the right rear out of the large room letting her long train drag on the floor to her left front. As she was going slowly backward, our Assistant Lieutenant Cranford, following her, backed too fast and stepped on her train causing a little embarrassment to both, and cautious amusement among the Princesses.

Usually after each such annual reception the wife of the Dean of the Diplomatic Group would ask the ladies, at least, to her home for tea. The purpose was to let the ladies look over each other's gowns. Following that tea, Gwynneth generally had a group of our friends in. We did not confine ourselves to the diplomatic Corps. All of the American women wanted to examine those court gowns. In all, it was always quite a day.

XIV
Distinguished Visitors

During our stay in Japan we met many interesting Americans who came over officially, as tourists, or for business purposes. Generally, they stopped at the Imperial Hotel but sometimes they were asked to be guests at the Embassy. They would be entertained by both the Japanese and the Americans and we would generally be invited to those parties. Sometimes we would be asked to help in their entertainment. In some cases it was our duty to take charge of the visitor ourselves.

For instance, one day the Ambassador asked me to go down to Yokohama and meet Mrs. Theodore Roosevelt, Senior, who was expected to arrive that day by liner. Of course, I went, met her, helped her through the Customs and drove her to our Embassy in Tokyo. She was just as interesting as she has been rated. Although in her seventies, she was still very lively both physically and mentally. In discussing our relations with Japan at that time she amused me by bringing up that celebrated old saying of her husband, "Speak softly but carry a big stick." Then I had to tell her the story of the visit of our big white fleet of sixteen battleships to Japan on their trip around the world as ordered by her husband in 1908. How they lay at anchor in Tokyo Bay off Yokohama for ten days while the officers and men were royally entertained by the Japanese government and people. I told her of the remarkable change in attitude of the Japanese toward us after that visit. And in the telling it was impossible for me not to bring in my own thrilling experience in going out on a big Japanese liner as the personal representative of the President of the United States, to welcome and review that great fleet as it came parading into Tokyo Bay with its bands playing, its many flags flying and its decks lined with sailors. You see the Minister had expected to go but that morning he had been summoned by the Emperor so he asked me to take over his duty. George V. Strong, a fellow student officer who lived with me in Tokyo went along as my Adjutant. We both had the important rank of Second Lieutenants at that time, but dressed in our fullest full-dress we looked from any distance just as ranky as any general or admiral, and George being from the Cavalry knew well how to make plenty of noise and how to strut his stuff and look important. He insisted on turning it on as it might impress people with my importance. We both were wearing our sabers. George let his hang low so that it would drag on the deck and ring against any obstacle encountered. That view of those sixteen white battleships in column passing before us could never be forgotten.

After that had passed and I had returned the salute of the last one, our liner hurried back to the Yokohama wharf while the fleet went to anchor. Quickly disembarking and taking rikashas, we started for the Yokohama railway station on our way back to Tokyo. We found the streets lined with Japanese school children. As we passed between their lines, they waved American flags, sang American songs and cheered us. Evidently we were thought to be Navy Admirals. It was embarrassing but at the same time quite amusing to us two fresh American

131

youngsters. Just once since then I have dared to tell that story in the presence of the Navy. It was at Philadelphia at a get-together dinner for the Army and Navy. The story evidently caused quite a stir at the Navy tables. When the Navy speakers who followed on the program had finished their stories there was not much left of Army Second Lieutenants.

Theodore Roosevelt II visited Japan on his return from a hunting trip in India. One evening, just as I returned from an afternoon at Golf, our maid told me that Mr. Neville, our Chargé d'Affaires, had been trying to get me on the phone. He had left word for me to come to dinner at the Imperial Hotel with Theodore Roosevelt. Quickly changing to a tuxedo, I hurried down to the hotel where in a private room Mr. Neville was host to a stag dinner party of some size in honor of young Teddy. Of course, I was at once introduced to the guest of honor. Taking the vacant seat at the table I said little but devoted myself to catching up with the others in my eating not only because I was hungry but because it was natural for me to want to listen to the drift of the conversation before taking any active part. It seems that Theodore was convalescing from some fever he had contracted in his hunting travels. He looked rather thin. I anticipated a quiet role on my part listening to the stories of the hunt. But I was in error. Soon I was the unwilling center of interest of the party. Suddenly, Teddy said in a loud voice for all to hear, "I can always tell when there is any person at the table with me who does not approve of me. There is one such person here tonight." The group became quiet and curious as they looked about the table trying to guess to whom he was referring. They insisted he should point out the guilty party since he had made the accusation. Dramatically he pointed his finger at me.

I was surprised as much as the others. Amazed in fact that he should have sensed my feeling. I thought that I had had enough diplomatic experience to conceal my feelings better than that. Now McIlroy was on the spot. Neville, as host, tried to keep the matter from becoming serious, and insisted jocularly that I tell them all about it. Teddy also insisted that I confess. So after keeping them in suspense for a time I said, "All right, all right. Since you insist I will answer the claim of our distinguished guest that I do not approve of him. In the first place I am amazed that he should get that idea. He probably mistook my quietness and apparent inattention caused by genuine hunger as disapproval. It is true, however, that ever since the World War my feelings have not been too kindly toward him. I cannot forget the derogatory statements he made in various political speeches against the officers of the regular Army. Such statements his father would never have made." Now the shoe was on the other foot. After a pause, his reply was to this effect, "Please bear in mind that those statements were made after the World War in political speeches." He then said something about wanting to drink me under the table. From then on he frequently raised his glass and insisted that I drink with him. At first, the situation worried me for I had never allowed myself to drink too much at any affair. But soon, I realized there was nothing to fear for in his weakened condition from his recent sickness he was in no form to drink anyone under the table. He soon slowed down with his demands that we drink together. That idea was probably just his way of showing that he wished to be friendly—that there were no hard feelings.

Later, he became Governor of the Philippines and we saw both him and his family in Japan several times. At parties I often sat next to Mrs. Teddy and Gwynneth often sat next to the Governor. Mrs. Teddy was quite a fine little woman. But Gwynneth never would admit that she liked the Governor. Now that wife of mine is not one given to gossip. If she can't say something good about a person, she will keep still on that subject. But when pushed by me in private, she said that the Governor was one of the most difficult persons to talk to she had ever met. That he would listen to nothing said to him unless it was about or in close relation to himself. In other words that he was extremely egotistical. Coming from her, that was certainly not to his credit. However, to do him justice in later years I heard from several sources that he performed well in World War II as a Brigadier General of the 1st Division, that he was recklessly brave and that the soldiers were very fond of him. He was killed fighting in Europe.

Another of our President's wives visited Japan during our time there. It was Mrs. Wilson. Gwynneth was at several parties with her. Mrs. Wilson was visiting her cousin, Dr. Teussler. The doctor was the head of the American St. Luke's Hospital. Gwynneth finally gave a luncheon for Mrs. Wilson. A little story may show something of her character. While she was at this luncheon of Gwynneth's she was asked to be sure to sign the guestbook before she left. She did overlook it but about an half hour later she returned and signed it with apologies.

When Patrick J. Hurley was Secretary of War in the Hoover Administration he visited Japan with his attractive wife. He had with him a young Medical Officer as his Aide. Gwynneth and I were asked to join them for a trip down to Kyoto and see them off on their boat for the Philippines. This was quite a treat for us. We found them a delightful pair. High class in every way. She was lovely in appearance and in character. He was a scream. Big both physically and mentally, full of amusing stories which he told well, he reminded me much of Will Rogers. In fact, he was reared in the same part of the United States as Rogers and knew him well. I was surprised that he should talk over with me the most confidential matters about both the political situation at home and the internal problems then bothering President Hoover. He seemed to hold back nothing. I had never been accustomed to having my superiors, even when on their staff, be so openly frank with me. I mentioned it to his aide and he said that he had noticed it and that it was unusual for the Secretary to do that. His explanation was that the Secretary had so much on his mind, and ever since leaving Washington no one with whom he could talk freely, and being convinced that he could depend on an experienced Intelligence Officer like myself to be discreet, he just unbosomed himself while thinking things over.

I recall his telling me about the various reforms in the Government for the general good which Mr. Hoover had in mind then but could not accomplish due to the antagonism of the then Democratic congress. He also discussed with me the important question of whom he should appoint as the next Governor of the Philippines. That was of especial interest to me as one of the persons he was considering was then my superior, the Ambassador to Japan, W. Cameron Forbes. He gave me to understand that Forbes had asked for a reappointment to that job. He had been Governor of the islands before and from all I have heard, a very good one.

It was interesting to watch Hurley as we went around sight-seeing especially in the temples and places. He was most careful to do that which he thought the Japanese would like to have him do under all circumstances. If a Japanese guide or interpreter took off his hat, a fraction of a second later off would come Hurley's hat. If a temple executive knelt before an altar Hurley's knees would reach the floor at almost the same moment. In the discussions with the guides the great military leaders (known as Shoguns) of the Tokugawa family would often be mentioned. They ruled Japan for two hundred years before the arrival of Admiral Perry in Tokyo Bay. Everywhere we went in Kyoto we heard so much about the powerful Shoguns. Finally Mrs. Hurley said one morning, "For a long time I have wanted some name to apply to this energetic husband of mine. Now I have it, I shall call him the 'Big Shogun'." We all agreed that the name fitted him perfectly. So thereafter, it was, "And now what is the pleasure of the Big Shogun?"

Whenever I hear Hurley's name mentioned today or see it in print I think first of him seated in the rear seat of a large open motor car with a big cigar in his mouth, telling the aide and me funny stories on our ride from Kyoto to Osaka one afternoon of our travel with them. For that trip, the ladies insisted on taking the train but the Big Shogun just as strongly insisted that the train for him would not do. So he had me secure for us three men a large open, seven-passenger car for the trip. It was a very sensible thing for him to do for the weather was pleasant and it gave him the opportunity to view the people of the country better than from a train window. As we rolled along through the small farms and little villages I explained to him the customs of the people, but half the time between big puffs from that immense cigar he was telling me funny stories. I thoroughly enjoyed that ride and I believe he did too.

Upon reaching Osaka we went directly to a small hotel where we had agreed to meet the ladies. There we four had a little supper with some bottles of Japanese beer and heard some more funny stories. Soon after they went aboard their ship on which they were sailing for Shanghai and the Philippines. Just before bidding me good-bye up on deck, he gave me a mission that was in a way an anti-climax to the trip. He said about as follows, "Now Colonel, I have a request to make of you. I wish you would tell Forbes that I have decided to appoint Theodore Roosevelt the next Governor of the Philippines." My reply was something to this effect, "It will not be a pleasant duty to perform but if that is your wish, your message will be delivered."

Upon returning to Tokyo I made it my business to complete that mission as soon as possible. The occasion was certainly embarrassing to me and I suspect that the news was not welcome to the Governor. It always seemed to me that the heart of Governor Forbes was still in the Philippines, his first love as it were. To me, he seemed to have a difficult time at first becoming thoroughly interested in his new job as Ambassador to Japan. Of course, I also realized that he had big financial interests back in the States that often demanded his attention.

On one of my trips to Peking I met a Mr. Crane, one of the brothers who owned the sanitary appliances manufacturing company that bears their family name. We were stopping at the same foreign hotel. I had come up from Tientsin with my sister and her husband. They introduced me to Mr. Crane. He had been Ambassador to China. After his relief from that assignment he interested himself in the investigation of the communistic movement in Russia. At that time, he was quite sure that it was a worldwide movement with the object of putting the Jewish race in political control of the world. This reminds me of a frank conversation I once had with a hitchhiker whom I picked up in Omaha on my way southward. He was a well-dressed Jew, a graduate of Harvard, and recently discharged from the Army. The subject of communism came up in our interesting conversation. I told him what I had found out in my own investigation of that movement in Eastern Pennsylvania and then told him what Mr. Crane had said to me about the movement. My companion was very emphatic in the statement he then made to me to this effect, "The Jewish people are naturally capitalistic. At heart no Jew is a communist. If you find them in a communist organization you may be sure they are there because they wish to get control of it, but not because they believe in it."

While in Peking at that time Mr. Crane was anxious to secure some really good jade. My sister introduced him to a cultured wealthy Chinese woman friend of hers who volunteered to be Mr. Crane's guide in his shopping for jade. They spent an entire morning at it coming in for a late luncheon. They asked us to join them for lunch. I sat next to the Chinese lady. When asked if they had had a successful morning, she replied enthusiastically, stating that Mr. Crane had invested rather heavily. As they had just come in I asked, "Well, what did you do with your purchases?" She patted her little bag on her lap and said, "Right in there." And then she showed me on her finger a large beautiful jade ring which she said Mr. Crane had given her. She was evidently quite happy over her personally conducted shopping tour of that morning.

Mr. Crane's chief pastime seemed to be cards. We enjoyed several evenings with him at bridge both in Peking and in Tokyo later.

An unusual couple of whom we saw much in both Peking and Tokyo was the Croziers. General Crozier was a retired Regular Army officer. He had been Chief of Ordnance at one time. He was noted as the designer of the disappearing gun carriage used much by our sea coast de-

138

fenses for years. He was tall with a kindly humorous side to him. Both were in their seventies but still very active physically and mentally. She was a fine-looking woman with a sharp inquisitive mind. It seemed they had been in love with each other for many years but for various reasons had not married until after the death of her mother and after his retirement from active duty.

They had been traveling the world over. It was difficult to name a single place they had not visited. In Japan and China, they had been making an extensive study of and collecting oriental art objects. They told me they had already sent to Baltimore for storage sufficient to fill a large museum. I wonder what was ever done with it, for I suspect from what I saw of their buying, it would be composed of very good things.

In addition to buying the best of oriental art, they interested themselves in international affairs. They were well informed apparently as much so as the average diplomat and always intent on learning more about the real facts of any matter under discussion. I always suspected that they were observers for the Secretary of State or even for the President of the United States. Anyway, they were a fine pair. We admired them very much.

The Lindberghs visited Japan on their trip to the Orient. Their arrival in Tokyo was a major event for that city. In fact, their expected visit had a strong effect on us some time before their arrival. As soon as the Ambassador learned of their intention to fly to Japan and China the question arose as to where they would live while in Japan. There was at that time no American government-owned Embassy, neither office building nor living quarters. Our Ambassador at that time, "Governor" Forbes, was living in a small but comfortable house in the Tsukiji section of the city which he rented from Dr.

Teussler, the head of the American St. Luke's Hospital. Other members of the Embassy staff were living in apartments or houses not well suited to receive such a noted couple as Charles and Anne Lindbergh. It was summer time and nearly all our families were at Karuizawa, the well-known summer colony up the mountains west of Tokyo. On one of my weekend visits to Karuizawa Gwynneth and I decided it was our duty to offer our house for the Lindberghs. The Counselor and Mrs. Neville immediately approved the idea.

Our home at that time was a large, part Japanese and part foreign-style, well-constructed house with a large beautiful garden and a private tennis court.

So I suggested the idea to our Ambassador. To my surprise, he insisted that if the Lindberghs stopped there we must turn the place over to them completely and stay away ourselves. When I reported the Ambassador's remark to Gwynneth she blew up. She emphatically insisted that if the Lindberghs came into our home they would come there with her, Gwynneth, as the hostess. She was not going to turn her home and furnishings over to anyone. So that was that. The result? When the Lindberghs were in Tokyo they were put up at the Teussler home.

I was especially interested in meeting Lindbergh because of the experience I had had in connection with him when we were still at Fort Benjamin Harrison, Indiana. While I was stationed at that post, Lindbergh had made his world rocking trip across the Atlantic. Soon after his return to the United States he began a tour in that celebrated *Spirit of St. Louis* which carried him to many of the large cities of this country. It gave the people a chance to honor their hero and him an opportunity to talk for avi-

140

ation. On that tour his quiet demeanor and evident unspoiled character won the hearts of the American people.

At that time I was a Major, commanding a battalion of the 11th Infantry. The morning of the day of his expected arrival at Indianapolis, I was suddenly presented the task of organizing a Provisional Battalion, of taking it to the air field of the city and of guarding Lindbergh until the city took him over. Well, I did organize the battalion, took it to the field and then placed a ring of sentries entirely around that field. However, I kept a small reserve with me at the main entrance to the field through which we expected Lindbergh to be taken to a waiting automobile for the drive to the city where he was to be given a luncheon and an opportunity to speak.

That reserve was largely composed of noncommissioned officers, mostly sergeants, all highly dependable men.

Of course when I posted the sentries they were given orders to keep all persons off the field and being Regular soldiers they would do that even if they had to be rough in carrying out their orders. However, soon came orders from my Regimental Commander, "You will instruct your sentinels to use no force." Wow! What a mission I then had. My instructions were to protect Lindbergh but my men must not use force. A peculiar situation in which a Regular Army unit should find itself. Naturally, I did not like it one bit.

Once before, that same commander in that same city had placed me in the same untenable position. That time I had been given a provisional battalion with which to protect the homes and property of a tornado-stricken section of the city and then told not to issue any ammunition, at least he said it would be my own responsibility if I did issue any to my men. Well, I did take the responsibility, issued the ammunition, and then had the Indianapolis papers publish the fact that our men were armed and ready to use any force necessary to carry out their orders to protect the property for which they were responsible. Well, nobody was hurt and we protected the property. In my humble opinion Regular Army soldiers should not be used for serious situations where it is expected that they will use whatever force is necessary to carry out their orders. The fact that it is well known that they will carry out their orders even if they have to shoot someone to do it—that fact well known—makes it unnecessary for them to shoot.

Coming back to the Lindbergh arrival, I realized that just as soon as that immense crowd lining the air field knew that those soldiers were there simply as a decoration, they would take advantage of it. So I asked the city police to let us have two dozen billies which were soon produced. I then trained my little reserve in how we would protect Lindbergh by forming a circle around him while holding on to our neighbor billies.

Soon Lindbergh and his *Spirit of St. Louis* showed up, circled the field and promptly and gracefully came in for a landing. He then taxied up to near where the reception committee was awaiting him. Before he was out of his plane the people had broken through my lines and were swarming toward his plane. Here my Sergeants and I went into action. Lindbergh stepped out of his plane and we hastened to surround him. Throughout his walk to the car awaiting for him, he conducted himself as though totally unaware of the dangerous situation he was in. We, however, did not feel so cool. We had to fight with all our strength, like a football team to keep the people from crushing in on him and the committee. I heaved a sigh of relief when he was safely into that automobile.

Turning the battalion over to the Senior Captain to take back to the post, I went on to the luncheon in Lindbergh's honor. It appeared that all were favorably impressed by his talk and generally unspoiled behavior.

Going back to Tokyo, the arrival of the Lindberghs in their own plane was an event not only to the Americans but to the Japanese as well. Everywhere they were acclaimed with much enthusiasm by the many people who lined their path. They were entertained magnificently both officially and privately. They took it all calmly. It would be difficult to find fault with any of their actions at that time. Gwynneth and I were invited to most of the affairs in their honor. Our Ambassador had them at his summer home in Karuizawa for a time. There we attended a small informal dinner for them. I sat next to Anne Lindbergh. She was an intelligent, interesting table companion. Charles Lindbergh seemed to have little to say at the table.

After the rush of entertaining was over, they settled down in the Teussler home in Tokyo with the announced purpose of getting some rest from the strenuous life. We were tipped off that it would be OK for us to call on them there. That we did. At that time we suggested their coming to our home for an informal luncheon with some of our friends who had not had the opportunity to meet them. They readily agreed. At the luncheon we had about ten of our most intimate friends. Again, I found Anne very charming and Charles very quiet and reserved. Later in Tokyo, we heard the criticism that Charles Lindbergh is too indifferent to people. That he is not interested in people at all. I am not prepared to answer that criticism as I do not know him well enough.

And now I come to the most distinguished personality about whom there has been so much discussion pro

143

and con. During the first period of our stay in Japan, Mac-Arthur was the Commanding General of the Army troops in the Philippines. He was then a bachelor or should I say a widower divorced from the daughter of the wealthy Stotesbury family in Philadelphia. I told you about his coming aboard our transport as we sailed from Manila for China. We did not see him again until 1931.

First came a letter from his aide telling me that the General would be stopping for one day in Japan on his way to Washington where he would become the new Chief of Staff of the Army. The date of his arrival in Yokohama was given me. Before replying, I called on the Secretary to the Minister of War and told him of the expected visit. Of course, to the Japanese he would be a visitor of number one importance. I naturally took it for granted that Mac-Arthur would make a courtesy call on the Japanese Minister of War at least, so I arranged with him as to the hour for that call. They immediately expressed their desire to give a large formal dinner for him. That too, was arranged and then I wrote the aide telling of the schedule I had arranged for the General after landing at Yokohama.

We heard nothing more until the day before the expected arrival at Yokohama. A telegram came from Kobe from his aide to this effect, "The General will be in Tokyo as a private citizen. He desires no official engagements made for him." Well—you can imagine how that upset me. The Japanese authorities had to be told that we would not call and that we would not accept the invitation for the dinner, which they had been preparing. The Japanese, of course, were surprised by his action and definitely wanted to know *why*. All I could say was that the General wanted to move about as a private citizen in Tokyo and again, the "But why?" would come out. I could not explain the sudden turn so did not really try to. It was a decided slap in the face for them. Knowing how tactful the General usually was, I could not think otherwise than that it was intentional on his part. It certainly put me in an embarrassing position as the two nations were supposed to be friendly at that time.

I realized that MacArthur's counterspy group in the Philippines had been keeping him well informed on the extensive and aggressive spy activities of the Japanese in and around the Philippines. He, no doubt, firmly believed that those high-ranking Japanese Army officers were enemies of our country and that he would sooner or later be openly fighting them. Perhaps he had some idea that it would be good psychology to show his indifference and contempt for them. I do not know. We can only guess his reason for that action. I hope he will explain it in his memoirs.

So I met him with my car at the dock in Yokohama. He and his aide rode back to Tokyo with me. In Japanese I gave instructions to the chauffeur to drive by the War Department on our way to the Imperial Hotel. As we were passing the War Department I said to MacArthur, "There is the office of the Minister of War if you should care to change your mind and call on him. I have no doubt that he is in his office now." His reply quietly given was, "Just take me right to the Imperial Hotel." There we sat in the lobby conversing. I was worried about what to do with him. Having a happy thought I asked him if he would like to have me get hold of as many of our student officers as possible and have them in for dinner with him at the hotel. That, he said, would be fine. So by phone I managed to bring five of the students and we had a pleasant dinner together talking mostly about the customs and the character of the Japanese people in which he seemed most interested. In fact, he put one searching question after another to the officers present to get their opinions and reactions.

After dinner, we took him on a tour of the beer and dance halls. It was always evident that he was studying the people in those places. Gradually the students and even his aide fell away and went home. About midnight the General and I were walking alone in a broad deserted street. Suddenly he stopped and said, "Now McIlroy, you run along home and I will go back to Yokohama." I protested leaving him to walk back alone to the station at least one-half mile distant. He insisted that I go, so go I did. And I have not seen him since.

Yes, that was an odd thing for him to do—to insist on walking alone to the distant station through the poorly lighted streets after midnight. Why did he do it? It is possible that he did not want to keep me up any later. He may have wanted that quiet walk alone to think over what he had seen and heard during the evening, to draw conclusions from it all concerning the Japanese. He might have also wanted to show the Japanese that he was not afraid of them even in their own country. Of course, every minute he was in Japan he was under the closest observation by skilled secret service personnel. They would not have permitted anything untoward to happen to him.

While we are on this subject of MacArthur, let me tell you of some other contacts I had had with him. It may show you other interesting sides to his character.

My first contact with him was as a new cadet at West Point in August of 1900. There were about two hundred of us—senatorial appointees, who had just reported for duty there. We were quartered in the old barracks facing the square. There was a large detachment of Third Classmen assigned to give us our basic training. In charge of that detail and of us was MacArthur, then the Senior Corporal

146

of the Corps of Cadets. Life was very hard those days while we were being disciplined and our posture corrected. The young corporals seemed to be everywhere making it just as tough as possible for us newcomers. But I never saw MacArthur himself stop a "beast," as we were called, and say anything unpleasant to him. Even then he was the dignified commander. To us he seemed like a god—so handsome, so erect, so immaculate in his uniform. Of course, we cadets saw him often and could not forget him but I was not conscious that he ever saw me but let us see.

After basic training was finished we were sent to join the Corps. Being five feet six and one-half inches in height I was sent to one of the center companies. MacArthur, being tall, belonged to a flank company of the battalion, so there was not much opportunity for either of us to see the other during those long winter months of concentrated academic studying. I was never conscious of his having seen me during that time.

But now it is June, academic studies are completed for that year. Our class has just been recognized as the social equal of the Upper Classmen. This first night of our new exalted social position there was to be a dance at Cullon Hall on the bank of the Hudson for the cadets. I decided to slip over and observe it from the balcony in order to know the ropes as I looked forward to inviting young ladies there for social affairs myself. So about eight o'clock that June evening I started over alone walking under the trees in the dim light of the old-fashioned gas street lamp posts. About one hundred yards ahead of me was another cadet walking over alone. Suddenly he stopped, looked back and called, "Come on, McIlroy, and walk over with me." It was MacArthur, and was I pleased. As we walked on he told me about the dances and he knew the subject

147

thoroughly for he was one of the cadets on the committee running those dances. This little act of his showed that remarkable memory of his and the kindly side of his character.

MacArthur had a remarkable career at West Point. He became First Captain, in command of the Corps Battalion, the head of the Hop Committee, which handled social affairs, played left field in the first baseball team, and standing at the head of his class academically, made a total mark for his four years, which had not been equaled for twenty-five years.

Our paths did not cross again until World War I in Europe. During most of my time overseas, I was an observer for General Pershing and as such visiting various parts of the American Sector in France including the frontline units to observe and report on conditions and situations as I found them. When something was discovered that needed correcting I had the power of General Pershing—that is, I could issue any order I thought advisable in his name and action would be taken at once. At most headquarters that I visited I had the feeling that I was not welcome. There seemed to be generally a fear of my presence although my real purpose was to help wherever I could. I quickly sensed this desire to get rid of me at most places. But the time I called on General MacArthur, my reception was totally different. He was that day fighting his brigade of Infantry in the front line in the battle of the Argonne. He was in a small but well-built French house near the front. The house and surroundings were as neat as a house and surroundings on a military post should be in peace time. He was back of a desk in the largest room, no sign of war around except the large map on the wall. He received me cordially, calling me by name as I entered, wanting to know at once what he could do to help me in my duty. In a few words he explained to me the situation of his brigade and his plans for the future. He radiated confidence in his ability to carry out those plans. Apparently he was holding back nothing. Of course, he made a splendid impression on me, which I naturally passed on in any report for the day.

XV
Travels

During my stay in Japan both as a student and later as Military Attaché, I traveled much. During those eight years most of Japan proper was gradually covered by me. Also, I made a number of trips to the Asiatic continent.

My travels in Japan as Military Attaché had a double purpose. One purpose was to see and become familiar with those parts I had not visited when a student. The other important purpose was to carry on my studies in connection with the report required of me on how to bomb Japan.

Many of my trips were arranged in connection with the inspection of some Japanese Army establishment. By careful selection of my route to and from, I managed to see many points of interest both from the standpoint of a military man and from the standpoint of a tourist. At the same time there was kept ever in mind my main mission—the study of how best to bomb Japan. Although I wrote nothing down for their spies to see, I gradually became convinced that the Japanese Army was aware of my main mission, for they began a steadily increasing effort to interest and train their people in the cities in the art of defense against the effects of bombing.

They probably discovered my main mission by observing that I frequently sat on the rear platform of the trains, by studying the maps that they would see me buy in various parts of Japan, and by noting that I had certain students under me live in the parts of Japan where there were important bombing. targets. For instance, on a trip to inspect a new arsenal in the southernmost island of Kyushu, I formed the idea in driving about that there might be a possibility of destroying the big steel plant or doing it great damage by bombing and breaking a dam in the hills nearby which held up a large lake of water. To study that possibility, I sent an officer of the Corps of Engineers to live near there for a time. But when he returned from that period of residence he reported to my disappointment that the Japanese had already made provision for directing the water away from the steel plant.

On one trip, I managed to stop over at the famous hot springs at Beppu in northern Kyushu on the southern shore of the Inland Sea. There it is where the bathers lay naked on the shore and cover themselves or parts of their bodies with the hot sand and mud. This heated ground is not caused by the sun but by the volcanic heat that comes up naturally at that point from the interior of the earth. While watching those rows of bathers, I realized that among them was an attractive foreign woman, a Russian was my guess. Suddenly she saw me. Like a flash she was up and hurrying to the bath house with her light kimono thrown over her. She had not minded the Japanese men bathers, but the one foreigner was too much. Later I walked over to a large open shed where there were about a hundred Japanese women bathing in the hot water and hot sand and mud. As I stood there observing the scene the Japanese women seemed wholly unconcerned about my presence, but soon I noticed one woman quite uneasy. I was not sure whether she was embarrassed by my presence or trying to flirt with me but I did note that she was not a full-blooded Japanese, but at least half foreign. Foreign women become accustomed to the nudist ideas of the Japanese. Neither one of those women mentioned was annoyed by a Japanese man in their presence—but a foreigner—that was wholly different.

On another journey I stopped at Fukuyama, south of Osaka, on a military post garrisoned by a regiment of Infantry. They put me in the saddle, let me watch their training, and turned out a review in my honor. Later in the afternoon at the officer's club I had a long conversation with the Japanese officers. One subject we discussed at that time was how to build up morale in one's military unit. They had me explain our methods and they told me theirs, which incidentally I already knew. They were most emphatic about the tremendous effort their officers had to make constantly to produce and maintain that morale and absolute type of discipline they required in their troops. They said they envied the ease with which the American officers could induce their soldiers to fight. Late that afternoon General Haraguchi showed up. He had been Japan's Military Attaché in Washington during part of the time I was on duty with the Military Intelligence Division there. He took me in his motor car to Tomo on the Inland Sea and thence by row boat to a nearby island where we had a Japanese dinner in an inn overlooking a magnificent view of the Inland Sea.

Let me tell you more about the General. He was in Washington during the prohibition days. He was at my home a number of times for dinner. Nearly always after he had departed, we would find behind our hall door a bottle of some excellent brand of whiskey. Little good it did me personally for some of my classmates who lived near found some way of knowing when Haraguchi came to my home and hardly would he turn the first corner after his departure when in would come those classmates to call and incidentally to sample (?) the contents of the latest bottle. He was known as the Christian General. He was the most knowable Japanese officer with whom I came in contact. Undoubtedly, he felt friendly toward Americans.

Some of my older readers may recall when four of our Army planes made the first round the world flight. It was quite an event for those days. Well, the State Department had been securing permission for that flight from the various nations of the world for many months. Everything appeared to the outsider to be all lined up and the pilots and planes ready but it did not start. Finally, one day I learned the reason. A young man from the State Department came in to see me. He said that he was at the end of his string and asked for a suggestion. My suggestion was that he forget the matter for a few days and let me have a try at it. He agreed. Immediately, I phoned General Haraguchi and asked him to meet me at the Occidental Restaurant on Pennsylvania Avenue at 1:00 P.M. He said he would be there. With me went the Major Eichelberger who was then on duty in my office. The General met us promptly. We ordered a luncheon that we knew a Japanese officer would enjoy. There followed a pleasant half hour of good conversation. When the General was filled with good food I became serious and began telling him why we had contacted him. We explained to him the unsatisfactory situation of our plans for the round the world flight. We told him how everything was ready except in Japan. I recall saying, "And you know, General, that Japan can no more stop this flight than she could keep the fleet of Admiral Perry out of Tokyo Bay. If your country insists on refusing us we will go by Siberia and China, and that will cause hard feelings here against Japan.

Now, we want you to come to our Air Intelligence office and we will show you all our plans for this flight. Nothing will be held back. Will you come?" He consented to go with us and that afternoon we had a long session with him in the Air office. Finally, he said, "Give me a few days and I think I can produce results." About two days later he phoned me that he was authorized to tell me that permission had been granted. Just an example of what can sometimes be accomplished through a personal contact even in the toughest organization.

One of my trips was to Nagasaki to see General Ford, the Chief of the Military Intelligence Division, who was passing through on an American transport. I took him to luncheon where we were served by geisha during our long talk. While returning to the transport, he bought and presented me with a malacca cane which I still have.

On that transport arrived Major Duty, his attractive wife and children. Duty stated to me that he was on a three-month leave of absence from the Philippine Scouts. After my return to Tokyo, he came into the office and offered to help me in any way I desired. Said he would rather be doing something useful than be idle during these three months of leave. His offer was gladly accepted. With his help, I began again quite a serious study of the Japanese Air Force. Finally, we turned out a series of reports for which I received a letter from the Far Eastern Section at Washington complimenting the office highly on our successful effort. You see all my efforts with Washington up till then to get an Air Officer even temporarily to help me were always answered in the negative and the excuse was that the officer would have to give up his flight pay. As I was living in Japan without that flight pay the argument did not impress me very much. Although the possibility was never mentioned between

154

Duty and me I supposed that MacArthur had arranged for that leave of Major Duty from Intelligence funds in the Philippines.

During this period of duty most of my travel in Japan was in the southern part during my early student days, even to include a tour of the northern island of Hokkaido where I visited the Ainus in one of their villages. Those prehistoric first settlers with their white skin and long beards are quite a contrast to the Japanese. Also, during my student days I made a number of long walks through the mountains. These mountain trips had been taken when I needed a real mental rest from the hard grind of daily study of that hardest of all languages. That luxury of mountain climbing I did not indulge in while there as Military Attaché.

Some of the places visited that I could recommend for consideration—places not on the usual list of resorts for tourists—are the following: the old crater of Akagiaan between Nikko and Ikao, Asama Yama near Karuizawa, Echigo Province in mid-winter, the noted Japanese garden at Takamatsu on the northen shore of the Island of Shikokuj, Tomo on the Inland Sea near Fukuyama, and Asonsan in the northern central part of the Island of Kyushu. Anyone who really wants to learn about the Japanese must get away from the large port cities with their foreign hotels, best even to get away from the railroads several times and take long walks spending the nights in good Japanese inns. In my student days we found it helped to take along some sweetened cocoa to fill out our breakfasts. The Japanese breakfasts in the interior are nothing to be enthusiastic about. They can become very tiresome.

And, of course, no real student of Japan should overlook the Sankei, the three most beautiful views in Japan in the opinion of the Japanese people themselves. One is Miyajima, easily accessible on the northern shore of the Inland Sea just west of Hiroshima. Another is Matsushima, north of Tokyo not far from Sendai on the Pacific. The third is Ama-no-hashidate on the shore of the Japan Sea to the north and opposite Osaka.

Throughout my eight years in Japan and extensive study at other times also, I naturally became quite well informed on that country. It was of course my specialty. When at parties at which Japanese officers were present it was not uncommon for some Japanese officer when asked a tough question about some part of Japan to say, "Don't ask me, ask Colonel McIlroy over there. He has been everywhere."

There is just no end to the interesting trips with beautiful scenery that one may take in Japan and it was an unusual trip indeed that did not bring one back with a better knowledge of that strange country and its people. For instance, there comes to mind the awakening I received from a visit to a school of the Tenrikyo religious sect near Nara. This trip was fitted in for us by our Japanese staff officer guides during the days we were attending the annual grand maneuvers near Osaka. There at the Jerusalem of Tenrikyo we saw a large well-equipped school for the training of missionaries to spread that religion over the world. Japan had its Shintoism, its Buddhism, its Confucianism and even some Christianity, but up to that time I had never heard of its Tenrikyo. Our lecturer claimed a following of five million members in Japan with hundreds of thousands in Asia and adjacent islands and thousands in North and South America. I quote from a letter of mine at the time. "They advocate bringing about a paradise here now on earth without waiting for a Heaven in the future. The originator of this

156

religion was a woman of forty-five who had been married and had children so was (they said) much better prepared to explain life than Christ or Buddha, who were younger, unmarried, and without much knowledge of life."

There is one other trip which I think deserves mention. It was by invitation to the celebrated Nikimoto Pearl Fisheries. It is on the Pacific well south of Tokyo. I was accompanied by Lieutenant Cranford, my assistant, and his wife. Gwynneth could not go because of the recent arrival of a new daughter in our family.

We were first taken out in row boats to observe the many Japanese girl divers at work bringing up the wire cages containing the oysters for inspection. This was followed by a lunch, which included oysters in some of which we found pearls. And after the luncheon we were each given a basket of oysters with which to amuse ourselves opening up the shells to see if they contained any pearls. Since we had been told before lunch to keep any pearls we found in any of the oysters, you can imagine what an interesting game it was. I had the luck to find a number of good ones which later in Tokyo I had mounted in a pin for Gwynneth. That night I spent at the house of Mr. Nikimoto. After retiring, I was awakened by strange flashing light. Opening my side doors I saw a most unusual sight, one that our Naval Attaché would have given his last shirt to have seen. It was the Japanese main fleet at anchor in the bay beneath me having night signal practice. As an ignorant Army officer, I did the best I could to take back to our Naval Attaché a description of what I had seen. Things like that do not happen by accident in Japan. But I could never figure out why I was taken there to see that fleet.

But now let us go to the mainland of Asia to Korea, Manchuria, and Northern China. In 1930 I decided to

157

visit those parts of the Asiatic continent to become familiar with the activities of the Japanese there. The last time I had really traveled in those parts was in 1910. I wanted to see what Japan had accomplished for herself in both Korea and Manchuria. Also, I wanted to visit my sister and her husband, Lieutenant Colonel Walter S. Drysdale, who was the Executive of the American Infantry regiment in Tientsin. And before returning, I expected to confer with the American Military Attaché in Peking.

So on October 1, 1930 I set out on quite an interesting trip. My first experience was an unpleasant one. My Japanese porter insisted on my taking berth number one over the wheels in spite of the fact that my ticket was plainly marked four. We almost came to blows for I was determined that no Japanese porter would push me around. At Yokohama a young captain and aide to some general came in and was assigned to number five. It was probably he who had insisted on a good berth. So when I would not move they probably took out the party in number five.

As I passed southward through Japan the truck gardens were full of women and a few men working early and late. Here and there they were beginning to harvest the rice. In that first-class car with me were mostly foreigners, for instance, a Mr. Potts from Los Angeles, a honeymooning couple, Kaul by name, from Pennsylvania with whom I had lunch. Also, a Mrs. Wilson whom I had met in Tokyo, and an English lord, very pleasant.

At Shimonoseki I had an hour's chat with Lieutenant Twitty, one of our language students whom I had living there. He liked the place so much that he requested an extension of his time there.

From Shimonoseki, I took the railway ferry for Fusan in Korea. There was but one foreigner aboard, an Englishman, but the steerage was full of Koreans returning to their homeland. At Fusan I put up at the Station Hotel, which was foreign-styled and fairly comfortable. Dinner I ate with the Englishman from off the boat.

And from now on I will do much quoting from the letters I wrote to my family at that time in Tokyo. These letters I hope will give an idea of how I combined the pleasure of a tourist with the duty of an Intelligence Officer seeking all possible information of the country in which he was traveling. I might add, however, that all the things I observed and learned were not mentioned in my letters as I realized that it was very probable that some of them might be opened and read before reaching my family. Or again they might be read by a spy in my own home when the family were out.

Fusan, Korea, Oct. 4, 1930—Am seated in a first class broad gauge American-type railway car in Fusan Station waiting to start for Seoul. Still peeved over the bum coffee they gave me at the hotel—strong and bitter with cold thin milk. That spoiled the effect created by the good apples and grapes and the German pancakes.

This is quite a different land from Japan. This city of 120,000 contains 40,000 Japanese who seem to have all the good jobs while the Koreans are leading the bull carts and doing all the heavy coolie work. One Japanese remarked to me that the Korean people are the poorest people in the world and judging from my observation here I would agree with him. The streets are full of pack carriers who stand around with two forked sticks on their backs. They can carry many packages piled one on top of the other and tied to these forked sticks. Everywhere women go about with big bundles on their heads. Their dresses are very full, loose, long and light.

Going through the city I saw many groups of Korean men squatting together. I wondered what they were play-

159

ing but found out that they were only talking. About what? I wonder. Wish I knew.

The dwellings here appear much like the Japanese but not so clean and orderly. The street cars run on a narrow 2 ½-foot gauge.

At last I saw my old friend the Chinese persimmon again—lots of them but smaller than those in Peking. Evidently, the Japanese do not permit them to be shipped into Japan to compete with their own.

Many Japanese officers and hundreds of school boys in uniform are coming over for the big maneuvers near and to the north of Fusan. This morning several hundred of those boys stood on the square in front of the hotel, took off their clothes, put on a supporter, and clean suit of underwear (BVD type), tied a red band about their heads, folded the heavy uniform in their furoshiki and marched off to maneuvers.

As we pull out of Fusan, I notice a back lot baseball field with goats grazing in it—not unlike the States. Now we are pulling up a valley between mountain ranges. Paralleling the railway track is a two-way gravel road. It passes over very weak looking bridges. It is lined with poplars. In fact, poplar trees are much used here about their homes and along the roads giving the general view a very French touch. There are rice fields everywhere. The 'roads' in all directions are full of pedestrians, all in white, going in all directions. Nearly every woman has a basket on her head and some have packs. The tall stove pipe like black hat seems to be the mark of a gentleman. The little villages in the hills are surrounded by stone walls. The walls of the houses seem to be either sonte or adobe and over all a thatched roof. On many of these roofs are growing big pumpkins with their spreading vines. Many also have a patch of red berries drying in the sun—just a touch of bright color.

Many of the houses seem to have but one room. The backyard of each house has about six large earthen jars sitting about, I suppose for holding water. The gardens are not neatly kept as those in Japan. Largely due to lack of water no doubt.

Just saw three women and a dog squatting along a small stream pounding away at a big washing. A big colorful market was in view for a minute. Am now going along a wide river with white sail boats on it. Most of the junks on the river seem to be really loaded with Koreans.

When in Fusan, I saw so many bulls that I wondered where could be the cows that produced them. Now I see they are up here on the hillsides grazing or in the paddy fields working. There are pine trees now and twisted and gnarled by the wind like those in Japan.

Some of the farmers along here wear a straw hat in the shape of a rather flat cone whose diameter at the base is about three feet. It protects from the sun and no doubt to some extent from the rain. I forgot to mention the Korean shoe made entirely of rubber with the Oriental turn-up at the toe.

All day we have been either in the mountains or in a narrow valley between them but now at 6:00 P.M. we find ourselves moving along through a wide valley with the mountains in the distance.

I see by the Seoul Press that there is a big gathering of all Americans in the city at the American Consulate this evening so I may attend that affair when I get in.

The Chosen Hotel, Keijo (Seoul), Oct. 5, 1930, 8:30 A.M. Too much coffee late last night, too many loud pounding church bells and temple drums, so I got up, had a shower, wrote Glen (brother) and now taking the pleasure of talking to my best girl.

Last night after securing this room, I walked out to attend the American reception at the American Consulate. I had a map to follow and did very well until an alley ended at a big iron gate. There I inquired of the gatekeeper where my nice map road was to the American Con-

161

sulate. He took me through a big estate, through a couple of gardens and then I saw the stars and stripes. The gate-keeper bowed very low over the fifty sen I gave him and then I entered the pretty place of a wealthy Korean, which had been turned over to the Consul.

There I found everyone enjoying the movies in an open garden—Jackie Coogan in *The Bugler*. About two hundred Americans including the children were present. They gave me a big white pasteboard box with big red and blue stripes diagonally across it filled with cold food.

I met Mr. Stephens, our Consul. He is to marry the daughter of an old resident here, Mr. Morris, who inciden-tally is to come to see me this morning and tell me tales I should know. After the movies were over and most of the guests gone a few of us collected in the living room of that quaint old home. It was chilly so I sat in front of the grate fire. They told me the grate and chimney had been de-signed and installed by Willard Straight when represent-ing the Morgan interests out there years ago.

So far I have seen three churches. I understand that there are as many Christians as anything else here. Con-fucianism is quite strong with a little Buddhism and Shintoism.

The Chosen Hotel, Oct. 6, 1930. A very full day yes-terday. Mr. Morris called for me, took me over to his office and talked me full of his experiences here. I had lunch with a Mr. Crane, Minister to China about 1921 when Walter (my brother-in-law) was there as Military Attaché. With us was a Mr. Saunders, companion of Mr. Crane, and professor of some Oriental school in Berkeley. Also, four Koreans, English speaking—all graduates of at least one American University. Crane is the bathroom fix-ture man. Lots of money.

After lunch a Mr. Oda, Sec. to the Governor General, came for us and motored us about town showing us the palaces, schools, etc., taking us into parts of the palaces

162

usually exempt to tourists. At odd moments of the day, I looked in at various curio stores, to learn about Korean chests. A good one of camphor wood of good color and grain with substantial brass trimmings will cost about 95 yen ($45). Late in the afternoon we attended a sermon by Bishop Welch at the American School Hall.

I dined with Dr. and Mrs. Noble, missionaries of thirty year's experience. A Mr. Williams of Standard Oil was also present. Heard many interesting stories. Returning to the hotel with Williams went in to have a night cap and found two drunken Americans trying to drink up all the booze behind the bar. At breakfast, chatted with Crane and Saunders. They are off by air for Darien and then by boat to Tientsin.

The Chosen Hotel, Oct. 7, 1930. Yesterday after writing you I walked over to the Consulate, talked to Stephens awhile, then took a taxi and called on the Commander of the Korean Army. He was quite a pleasant Japanese. Returning to the city I walked about looking at Korean chests and observing the soldiers marching hither and thither getting ready for the big maneuvers. Lunched with Mr. Stephens and his prospective father-in-law, attended to business at the Consulate and about four we went to the golf course for nine holes. Returning I was introduced to the crowd at the club. Stephen had dinner with me at the hotel. Much has happened about which I cannot write. ********** Must pay bill now and then away for Antung on the border where I will probably sleep and take an early train for Mukden.

Enroute Keijo to Antung, Oct. 7, 1930. Took no breakfast in the hotel dining room because of the lack of good butter, coffee, and milk. Instead had a big glass of good milk at the bar for 35 sen (18 cts.), a 10-sen piece of chocolate, and an apple. At the station the Governor's Secretary introduced me to a Mrs. Cushman and a Miss Scott, her niece from New York going around the world. They have managed to while away much time. Apparently, very nice people.

This country is so different from Japan and southern Korea. More like China and in places like America. No more rice but wheat, beans, kowliang (like corn). Most of the crops have been harvested. Soil is red clay. Country is rolling with a mountain range in the distant east.

4:40 P.M. Just saw a funny thing. At our last stop outside our window was a muddy stream which flowed under our track and the adjacent switch. Both were supported by a wooden bridge. On the outer edge of that bridge was a two-inch plank on edge. Trying to walk that plank just outside my window was a young Japanese school boy. He was in the usual black school uniform with his books in a knapsack on his back. As I was watching him he lost his balance fell outward across a switch wire about two feet from the bridge and then down into the muddy stream beneath. Two Korean men rushed to help him but soon they broke out into a hearty laugh for the boy was climbing out, all wet and muddy evidently sadder but wiser. Soon all the railway men in sight were enjoying the incident. Wonder what his mother said in Japanese when he arrived home?

There are orchards along this railway with red apples on the trees. They do not shock their kowliang as we do our corn. You know we make a large circular shock but they first make large bundles of their tall kowliang fodder and then lean two bundles against each other. Then by placing other pairs of bundles alongside they form a long line with an inverted V-shape space beneath through which one could walk erect. The farther north I go the further advanced is the harvesting. Up here near the Yalu there is much rice. Nearly all of it is cut and standing in sheaves on the elevated narrow paths between the paddies. I have seen two Manchurian ponies. One was run-

164

ning away with a long rope dragging—so typical of the peppy fat little things.

Enroute Antung to Mukden, Oct. 8, 1930. And now it is Manchuria—no more Korea. The change took place at the Yalu River and it was certainly a real dividing line. On the east side, all Korean, with white clothes. On the west side, all Chinese or Manchus with their black or dark blue clothes. Houses, clothing, crops, customs, trees, all changed. Here we see the little round caps with the little ball on top, the long gray brick huts so close together, much corn, some opium fields, many trees of various kinds, the bridges with their stone and concrete guard houses, now and then two to four Japanese soldiers along the track, wagons in the fields and along the dirt roads drawn by two cows, one pony and one little donkey, a drove of black razor-backed hogs in a field, a blue-jacketed Chinaman with two donkeys scampering along after him like dogs, wheat and corn in big shocks, coolies working on the tracks in blue clothes with big patches all over them in various shades of blue, the big hills and mountains, now near now distant, with their autumn foliage of all colors, fewer houses on the farms, bigger and better walls about their houses which are more prosperous-looking than those in Korea, in the barn yards huge stacks of fodder.

For the first time on this trip I find my car well filled, mostly German and Japanese with but one Chinaman.

There are remarkably few farm houses here and the fields are often large like our own. Little or no truck farming like one sees so much of in Japan. There goes a big cart with a load of fodder bound on it—almost as large as we would have on our big four-wheeled wagons. It is drawn by a pony near the load assisted by three donkeys ahead and abreast.

The guarding of this railway—the soldiers and blockhouses—is an interesting study. The blockhouses are

165

usually at the entrance to tunnels and at each end of the bridges. Some made of stone and concrete look like small castles. Some are circular with the lower part made of stone while on top is a steel turret. All types have many openings through which rifles and machine guns can be used. Near one station was a large rectangular block house with circular turrets at diagonally opposite corners.

The scenery is really quite beautiful—the mountains with all their fall colors, the willows and locusts near and the fields full of kowliang in rows with their deep red tops. There is an evergreen tree here that is really not ever green. Right now it is turning yellow and losing its needles. In some places they have planted whole fields of those evergreens on the mountain sides. There goes a cart with three ponies and one mule pulling it.

Just caught a glimpse of the old train I rode on through here in 1910. Cars were as long as they were wide with a very narrow gauge.

Pulling into Mukden now after leaving the mountains behind and then crossing wide level plains.

Mukden Club, 9 Oct. 1930. This is a large rather good club. ***** Well, where did I leave off? On the train somewhere near Mukden or Hoten as the Japanese call it.

Arriving at 1:00 P.M. I went to the modern Yamato Hotel, took a small but very convenient room with most modern bath, which is appreciated. Soon I was in a rikasha headed for the American Consulate, riding through the modern-looking Japanese New Town with its mixture of Chinese, Lloyd Wright, and Russian-style buildings. From a distance I could see the high flying American flag but when I arrived at 1:40 P.M., although the offices were all open, I could raise no one. So in my rikasha I went for a long ride to the Old Town, which I saw first twenty years ago.

How I wished you were with me. You would have enjoyed the strangeness of it but believe me you would have felt like being disinfected afterwards. I walked a long way, stopping now and then to look into strange shops. The most interesting ones were those filled with furs. Skins of every animal found in Asia were hanging close together from the wooden rafters and on projections from the front of the shops. Fur shops everywhere—whole streets of them—I never saw so many furs in all my life—tigers, bears, wolves, dogs, cats, squirrels, rabbits, foxes, and of course, many that I could not identify. At some stores they were having auctions. I recall one beautiful evening wrap with a blue rich brocade on one side, a brown and white mixed fur on the other side with a white fur collar. Looked like a million dollars. But I am told that Tientsin is the better place to buy.

The Chinese seem to have gone crazy over bright colored modern things. In many shops were displayed bright colored cheap foreign pictures with wide red frames on them, many modern mirrors with giddy-colored frames, and thermos bottles with bright pictures on them. With everything—houses, stores, clothing, the dirt of the streets all dark and somber—it is no wonder they seek some bright colors.

In the streets everywhere are roasted hazelnuts for sale. For transportation they have bicycles, rikashas, old Russian carriages, carts, and a few automobiles. Those old carriages are beyond description. Left here by the Russians in 1905, never washed or painted since, repaired just enough to keep them moving, wheels wobbling, making tracks like snakes, the harness in such condition that you expect it to drop to the ground any moment, a funny coolie driver on the front seat, three or more Chinese in the back seat, with much wild-looking baggage piled between and on top, and all pulled by a little rough-coated Manchurian pony. Among the many Chinese one sees here and there a Japanese and a few Russians. The latter are far from prosperous in appearance, wearing funny clothes, the woman sad and weary looking, but some of the children are bright and attractive. Over it all a cloud of dust—dirty dust—filling your mouth, eyes, nose and ears. And the filthy ragged beggars should not be forgotten.

Returning to the Consulate at 3:30 P.M. I found the Vice-Consul Lynch, who took me with his wife to the golf course for a little while. Later, they dropped me at the hotel. After cleaning up I went over to the club where Lynch met me again and introduced me to a number of people who were dancing and playing cards.

Strange to say they eat here between 9:00 and 10:30 P.M. For dinner parties people send out invitations reading 8:15 P.M. but do not expect their guests to arrive before 9:30. That gives everyone a chance to enjoy club life between office hours and dinner. For the dancing they had a good Russian jazz orchestra. At the hotel for dinner there was also good Russian music.

Later Mr. and Mrs. Mitchel took me home with them. I saw a large beautiful home, inside at least, with much well-selected Chinese furniture—the long hall stands, the tall square stands, etc., with Peking and Mukden rugs. The latter are about one third the price of the Peking rugs and quite OK for halls and bathrooms.

Rikashas here cost 20 sen (10 cts.) an hour. Caddies want 20 sen for eighteen holes. Did I tell you about the caddies stripping themselves at the water hazard to be ready to get Mr. Morris' ball out of the water at Keijo? Ask me when I return. It was really funny.

This morning I called at the consulate, met and chatted with Mr. Myers, our Consul-General, called on the Colonel commanding the 33rd Japanese Infantry regiment, and on General Suzuki, who is on the staff of the Japanese Manchurian Army. They are having maneuvers all along the railway but I was not asked to join them.

Everywhere I find the Japanese very pleasant. They

168

certainly are improving the looks of this country with their buildings and roads.

The letter describing the happenings on the 10th of October is missing from my files. It was a day of unusual experiences for me. The main events all centered about the young ruler of Manchuria, Marshal Chang Hsiao Liang and his family. There was the luncheon given by the Marshal, the review of the Marshal's troops, and a late supper dance at his villa.

The day was given over to the celebration of the appointment of the Marshal to the position of—was it Vice Commander of the Chinese Army. You see at that time Chiang Kai-shek was extending his power over all of China as he steadily worked up from the south. When the Marshal accepted this new appointment it meant the union of Manchuria and China Proper.

As a guest at the luncheon I was at the table of the Marshal and seated almost opposite to him so I had an excellent opportunity to observe him closely. The object of the luncheon was the public acceptance by the Marshal of that appointment.

At the review in the afternoon I had another opportunity to observe the Marshal. Some of his ladies were also present. Of course, I was greatly interested in seeing his Chinese troops for the first time. It was quite evident that he had put a lot of morale into them. They were neat and they marched well with their little ponies, but I was decidedly not sure of their fighting qualities. Both in ranks and on the streets off duty the Chinese officers and men appeared quite cocky and sure of themselves. That attitude especially in their presence did not please the Japanese officers. There was no doubt that the Marshal had in view the securing of control again of the railroads and towns then in the hands of the Japanese. One had the feeling that he was near a powder keg that might blow up at any time.

For the supper dance I received the following invitation:

Marshal and Madam Chang Hsiao Liang request the pleasure of your company at a supper dance in their Peilin Villa at 9:30 on the evening of the National Day, 10th of October, 19th year of the Republic.

That evening was a rare experience. Present were many Chinese officials, officers, and their families, foreign consuls and their families, and many foreign businessmen and their families. I heard many rumors about the ambition of the Marshal to run the Japanese out of Manchuria, rumors about the Marshal indulging in opium, rumors about the Marshal's concubines, etc. In all, it was a day long to be remembered.

Yamato Hotel, Mukden, 11 Oct. '30. Ten o'clock and just back from breakfast. My table companion was a White Russian, honorary Consul for Portugal in Harbin. On my way through the lobby I ran across the Turkish Ambassador and the Madame, both looking so well, especially the latter. They are returning from Peking. Today I am taking it easy departing on a 4:00 P.M. train for Harbin.

Enroute Mukden to Changhung, 11th Oct., 8:30 P.M. Almost at Changhung, the end of the Japanese-controlled line. There we must change to the Russian-controlled line and ride all night arriving about 8:00 A.M. at Harbin. The trip up this afternoon has been quite uneventful. On both sides a wide level plain with an occasional Chinese town

170

and corresponding to it directly on the railway, a small Japanese town built of red bricks.

This afternoon I saw many brick kilns. They are made apparently of brick covered over deeply with earth and surrounded by deep wide holes they have dug through the years. Here they make that gloomy gray brick so much used throughout China. Here also I saw for the first time on this trip those extensive fields filled with grave mounds, in other words the cemeteries of the Chinese people which in some parts of China take up such a large portion of the much needed land. The body is placed in a wooden box on the ground and then a mound of earth piled over it. The bigger the mound, the more important the deceased I suppose.

Harvest here is long past and even the stubble has largely been taken in. Frequently I see flocks of thousands of crows. On the train are a number of Russians. It seems strange to see so many white women, most of them very white skinned and rather fat.

Sunday morning, 12 Oct. 9:00 A.M. In funny old Russian hotel. Have had breakfast with very black coffee. Have some rubles in my pocket and am now going to try to find young Page our Vice Consul here. The sun is shining and not too cold but very windy and dusty. It seems strange to deal with big white waiters.

Enroute Harbin to Mukden. Oct. 14. '30. Writing in the observation car. Must use pencil in preference to their bum pen and no ink. The road is quite rough so do not expect much. I have just had breakfast in the diner. Seated opposite me was a slender little English girl, apparently the stenographer of the man and wife at the next table.

Well, Harbin was certainly worth a visit. So different from any other place I have seen. There are about two hundred thousand white people there. Among them many big upstanding fellows with high black boots—and beau-

171

tiful women to spare. Of course plenty of Chinese and then all grades between the two such as Tartars, Buriats, etc. It seemed strange to have white chauffeurs and waiters and even white Russian porters. Much of the city is foreign in appearance with fine buildings of white stone everywhere. There are many interesting stores, big ones too, where you can buy almost anything, such as good long neckties, and Arrow shirts, for five yen ($2.50). There are quaint old pawn shops containing priceless old Russian things.

Russian food was wonderful and very cheap. For instance, last night the bill for three of us after a delicious dinner with a martini, lots of draft beer, hors d'oeuvres, soup, meat and dessert was $14.00 Mex about $3.00 gold. Each course was a delight—big helpings and the flavor something to remember.

Had a ride in one of the Russian old time droskys. In Harbin they have removed the top or perhaps they just dropped off from dry rot. Large horses are used here so their appearance is even funnier perhaps than in Chanchung. Wherever the rubber tires have worn out they have inserted what appears to be chunks of rubber wired together. A long ride in one cost me 20 sen (10 cts.).

I must tell you about my hotel room. It is quite large with very high ceiling but very unattractive. It contains an unusually large bed, a very tall and slender clothes hanger imbedded in one wall, several small straight-backed chairs, much wicker furniture, and no rugs. The floor consists of wide hard boards painted. The ceiling and walls are painted with wallpaper designs. Plaster is falling off in places. There is one circular table and a wash stand over which there is a square tank of water. Out in the hall was a single toilet for use by both sexes. The plumbing reminded me of my boyhood days around 1890.

Before I forget it they say here that the Japanese

learned to handle their toothpicks from the Russians and I can easily believe it.

Well, I found Page in bed after a Saturday night party. He dressed and we walked over to the Consulate, quite a respectable place. We found the Acting Consul, Thomas, in bed also. But they got busy and showed me conditions, having that day and the next people in to talk to me, all of which was most worthwhile. Some funny characters I will tell you about.

I lunched there in state with Thomas. Later I joined a party at an English banker's apartment. He had married a beautiful Russian, who kept several of us men entertained. They had a horse in the races that afternoon so all of us went out there—an unusual experience. Later Page and I spent some time at the club, then had a splendid dinner and later to a cabaret returning to my hotel about midnight.

The next morning I spent in real work at the Consulate and lunched as guest of Page at the Hotel Moderne with a Mr. Ott of Standard Oil. In the afternoon, I took a long walk and then rested in my room until 8:30 P.M. when I went out to a good dinner with Page and an American businessman. Be sure to ask me about the Russian food and the way they serve it. Also ask me about the grand sleeper I rode on going up to Harbin. Best I was ever in. Beautifully finished in bright cherry with brass finishings and with every possible convenience.

In this train this morning are many families returning from Europe—all nationalities. They reported a comfortable trip with plenty of food.

Shanhaikwan, 15 Oct. 10:00 A.M. Yesterday I arrived at Mukden at 2:00 P.M. After waiting impatiently for forty minutes I learned that I could not buy my ticket and berth for Tientsin for the 9:40 P.M. train before 9:00 P.M., so I took a rikasha for the Consulate. After a chat there I went up to the club to pay my bill but the manager was not in. I then called on the Lynches, who were not at home; then on the Consul-General and his wife with whom I had tea. Returning to the club I had cocktails and renewed my acquaintance with Mrs. Li, the wife of the social secretary of Marshal Chang, Mr. Elder, one of the Marshal's advisers, Hutton, the Ford plane man, Mrs. Mitchel, the wife of the American Ordnance Expert, the wife of the Italian Consul, the wife of the American Trade commissioner, and a couple of Standard Oil men. I ate my dinner alone at the Yamato Hotel and walked to the station.

This trip down from Mukden is certainly an experience but not exactly a pleasant one. The cars are quite old, rather dirty, ugly, with almost no conveniences. Towels, hot water, paper, etc. apparently are not a necessity to the Chinese. Almost everyone is two in a compartment so being alone in mine gives me something to be thankful for.

There are a number of English and French aboard but no Americans. In the next apartment to mine the French family has a large female German police dog. Last night it was very cold due to there being no heat on because an armored car had been placed back of the engine for protection against bandits. They say only yesterday they had trouble with bandits in the country through which we passed last night. There are many armed officers, soldiers and police aboard. This morning from my window I saw flocks of pigeons, black birds, and a few cranes and crows.

As we approached and entered Shanhaikwan this morning I had again a very good view of the Great Wall and also of the many forts on the hills to the north on both sides of the railroad. You would have been amused at the way the Chinese got their breakfast at the Shanhaikwan station. On the platform were sellers of every conceivable kind of food and much of it hot. There were biscuits, broiled ducks in baskets, large bunches of large grapes, cakes, eggs, hot drinks, apples, pears, persimmons, etc. As for me I ate a bum breakfast in a dirty diner beside a

174

Chinese Major who talked a little Japanese and a little
French—by name Goa Fung Tsu—don't try to remember
it.

At Tientsin I visited with my sister whose husband
was a classmate of mine at West Point, Colonel Walter S.
Drysdale. They had a large comfortable apartment filled
with high class Chinese furniture, rugs, and art objects.
My sister was an expert on Chinese things. She had lived
with me in Peking during the winter of 1904 and 1905,
had spent another four years in that city while her husband had served as Military Attaché to China, and now
he was the Executive of the 15th Infantry stationed in
Tientsin.

I made good use of my sister's shopping knowledge
during the two days with them in that city. We searched
the shops and welcomed the Chinese salesmen at her
apartment with their packs of interesting things to display. One evening we went to dinner at the home of the
Chen family of four. We sat around a circular table covered with the best of Chinese food, all of which we enjoyed. The four Chens, including their two attractive
daughters, spoke excellent English. This experience impressed me with the difference between the Chinese and
Japanese. Had my sister and her husband visited me in
Tokyo at that time, no high-class Japanese family would
have thought of asking us all in for a family dinner. It
would have had to be a formal dinner with many others
present.

On the 16th I attended a review of the 15th Regiment
given for General Charles King.

Peking, 7:30 A.M., Sunday, 19th Oct. 1930. Am now at the
home of Dr. Shoemaker, head of one of the big rug firms

175

here. We are stopping here as guests because we were unable to find rooms in any of the hotels which are loaded with tourists.

Dr. Shoemaker is a former missionary who turned to business. He has a lovely foreign-style house filled with beautiful rugs and old art treasures with a pretty garden all surrounded by a twelve-foot wall covered with a creeping vine. At present, I am seated in that garden under a trellis covered with wisteria which is trained along a projection on the garden side of the house. In front of me is a little fish pond into which a tiny stream of water flows with the pleasant tinkle of a small waterfall. To my left are stone walks and grass plots bordered with flowers. To my right is a small swimming pool surrounded by slender evergreen trees and large rose bushes full of bright red roses. I didn't know that such a fairy land ever could be found in Peking. It is so much more luxurious than anything I ever saw in their palaces.

We came up to Peking by car, ninety miles, with Walter driving. Mr. and Mrs. Chen came with us. We followed a broad dirt road lined with willow trees. It took us four hours including a stop for tea on the roadside. While we were eating an old farmer and his sons came near to watch us. We gave them various things. They seemed to enjoy it all. Funny to see them wondering which part of the bananas and oranges to eat and how to eat them. At one place, we found a two-foot wall across the road, apparently built by bandits. Near Peking and in certain streets of that city we found raised places across the road used I was told to force motorists to drive slowly. They are dangerous for they can scarcely be detected at times.

Unfortunately, this is a poor time to shop here with all these tourists in town but I am doing my best with Lois's help. Of course, I need about 50,000 more dollars to do it right, but anyway I have picked up considerable costume jewelry, a neck piece of two stone martins, a jewel box, some very pretty Chinese women's wearing apparel, and two small rugs. For myself I have had made a gray Oxford tweed coat and some white flannel trousers. For Garfield (my son), a gray suit.

I saw here a better made imitation Korean chest, size 56 by 33 inches for 80 yen. It has much drawer space including three at the bottom for linens—at the Peking Craft Shop. Ten yen additional for lining the drawers. I am still looking for a hall table, candle sticks, jade, pajamas, etc. Lois says her evening shoes cost her only $2.00 gold.

Saw Bishop Reifsnider last evening at the Peking Hotel. Must go into breakfast now with the others.

Will continue indoors as I find only the tow-headed children up so far. Last evening we spent with Mr. Crane at the hotel. You will laugh to know that I found our celebrated Mrs. ——— in the Shoemaker show rooms selling to tourists and feeling very important.

Lois (my sister) thoroughly enjoys running around helping me shop but it is difficult to keep her mind on the things for which you asked. They have more or less contempt for all things Japanese. Of course these elaborate Chinese things are beautiful. And if a thing is old and dirty-looking they will pay more for it.

The old folks are coming in now. We eat on the closed veranda. Nearby are two love birds making me homesick. There is also an amusing parrot trying to get our attention by tearing up pieces of paper and loudly squawking.

While in Peking, my sister, her husband, and I were entertained at luncheon by the American Military Attaché, Lieutenant Colonel M.A. and Mrs. Margetts. They were most fortunate in having been able to rent a fine foreign residence.

In Peking we three were very much at home for in 1904 and 1905 my sister and I had lived in that city in the Legation Guard compound, and just after World War I,

Colonel Drysdale and my sister had lived there while he was the Military Attaché.

My return to Tokyo was made by boat from Taku, the port of Tientsin. I brought with me many beautiful things and shipped the heavier articles by freight. So my return was welcomed like the coming of Santa Claus.

Formosa and the Mandate Islands were not visited by me. It would have been difficult if not impossible to secure permission to visit Formosa and I knew that if they did let me go I would not be permitted to get near any of their military installations. And as for going to the Mandate Islands, that was totally impossible. Even non-military Americans could not go there.

Part 2
Second Period,
September 1931–March 1933

XVI
Beginning of World War II

On September 18, 1931, the Second World War began. That may seem to some to be an exaggerated statement but I could quote a number of authorities with the same conviction. That night of the 18th and 19th of September the Japanese Army began its long-planned aggressive moves to take over the Orient. Her unopposed success encouraged Mussolini and later Hitler.

That morning of the 19th of September when I awoke I reached as usual for the *Japan Advertiser*, that excellent morning paper published by the American Fleisher family. There in big type was the announcement that Chinese troops had blown up the Japanese-controlled Manchurian railway just north of Mukden with the intention of wrecking the evening express from Changchun to Mukden. It also stated that the Japanese, unable to stand for all the sabotage of the Chinese, had retaliated by seizing the Chinese-controlled Mukden arsenal and attacking the local Chinese troops.

Immediately after breakfast I went down to the office of the Embassy where I found that our Ambassador, Mr. Forbes, had planned to leave Japan the next day for a short business trip to the United States. The question was should he go now in view of the Mukden incident? He seemed to think that there was little that he could do to help the situation by remaining in Japan at that time, so decided to go as planned. As I did not know what was taking him home, I felt that it was not up to me to advise him. Also, I thought that Mr. Neville and I could do all that might be required in his absence. Recently a relative of his blamed me for not keeping him in Japan. Apparently, he must have been criticized for leaving Japan at that time for he came back in a hurry.

As soon as the Ambassador had left the office I had a talk about the situation with Mr. Neville. I told him with much satisfaction that I already had my assistant, Captain Cranford in Mukden and that no doubt we would soon receive a telegram from him about the situation. Naturally, we both doubted the story that the Japanese Army had put out about the whole affair.

You may remember that Captain Cranford handled the political and economic information for my office. About a month before he had warned me that something was liable to break in Manchuria in the near future. So I had permitted him to go to Mukden about the 8th of September, ostensibly on a pleasure trip. After the incident we waited impatient from day to day for some word from him. We supposed he was having difficulty in getting off his telegram. Finally, after ten days word came from him in Peking saying that after being in Mukden for ten days he came to the conclusion that the Japanese Army would start nothing while he was there so he had decided to slip over to Peking to talk the situation over with the Military Attaché there. The Japanese had started their action just as soon as Captain Cranford had sailed from Darien for Tientsin. Of course that was a big disappointment to me. We found out later that there was not a single foreigner with any military knowledge in Mukden on the night of the big incident.

From then on I realized that I was in the important spot of our national intelligence system. No instructions came to me at that time from my government, but I knew that it was up to me in some way to keep them informed in Washington about the mobilization of the Japanese Army and concerning any troop movements in Japan or to Manchuria. It was presumed that the War Department in Washington would be receiving information from the Military Attaché in Peking about all Japanese troop movements in Manchuria. From the reports of the two of us a close estimate of the military situation and the future intentions of Japan could be arrived at by the Military Intelligence Division in Washington.

Of course, the Army Intelligence group of the Japanese War Department would do all they could to prevent my securing accurate information about the location and movement of the Japanese troops. My increased activities soon brought about a quite noticeable difference in the way the officers of the War Department and the General Staff greeted me. It was at this time that our Secretary of State, Mr. Stimson, began sending those sharp notes to the Japanese government. The Army blamed me for having influenced Mr. Stimson in his critical attitude. They knew I was sending many reports of the facts, which were not favorable to Japan.

Gradually but definitely the Japanese officers became less friendly. It took them longer and longer to answer my letters of inquiry, which were generally submitted officially as a result of instructions from our War Department to ask the Japanese Army for certain information about—well, some minor weapon for instance. It would take several calls at the office of the Japanese Military Intelligence or perhaps the War Department before I could hope for a reply and even then, the information granted me would be very meager and unsatisfactory. It was quite evident that they were not going to cooperate with me as long as I insisted on being so energetic about sending to Washington the facts not favorable to them.

In Chapter X, I wrote of my unsuccessful attempt to persuade our War Department to treat the Japanese Military Attaché as I was being treated. Now it happened, my predecessor, Colonel Burnett, was assigned to that contact duty in the Military Intelligence Division, handling our Military Attachés abroad and maintaining contact with the foreign Military Attachés in Washington. He wrote me that he would do his best to put over the idea of treating the Japanese Military Attaché just as they treated me in Tokyo. I do not know how successful he was in carrying out that plan. I doubt if he got very far for when I returned from Japan I found that the officer-in-charge of all our military intelligence had been on very close social relations with the Japanese Military Attaché. I would bet ten to one, if it were possible to prove it, that that shrewd Japanese officer derived much more from that relationship than we did.

Well, how did I keep track of the Japanese troops? One of the first things I did was to call in my seven or eight student officers and tell them that in reading the Japanese papers to look out for any reference to troops, as units or individuals, and to furnish me informal translations of such bits of information. They were also to observe carefully and report any movement of troops seen by them. They were to note and report identifying insignia seen on individual soldiers. In their association with their teachers and other Japanese they were to be on the lookout for information concerning any soldier home on furlough.

184

Mrs. Neville, the Counselor's wife, remarked to me one day that her husband had told her that he was amazed at the knowledge I had of the whereabouts of the Japanese troops.

In the meantime, Japan was slowly but steadily taking over all of Manchuria. One day I had a long talk with Mr. Neville, telling him how serious I thought this movement of the Japanese Army was. He gave me the feeling that he did not consider it as serious as I did. His oft repeated argument was that Japan could not long sustain any real offensive because she did not have the financial strength to carry through. My reply to that was that any nation could fight a war as long as they could buy or seize the supplies necessary for carrying on their activities. His idea seemed to be that inside a year the Japanese would be trying to get out of their costly venture. I declared to him most emphatically that the Japanese Army in my belief was out to take just as much territory as possible and that nothing but superior force would stop them. Finally, I said, "I think that I will go back to my office and write the War Department my convictions concerning this matter." Mr. Neville replied in words to this effect, "Go to it Mac, but remember this—a democratic government like ours, due to frequent change of party and personnel, cannot carry out a consistent foreign policy for any time. But go get it off your chest, it will do you good. Someone will read it with interest, but I fear it will then be filed and forgotten."

Well I did return to my office and after thinking the situation over again from all sides and studying the map of Asia again, I wrote what I considered a very important letter to the War Department accompanied by a map to illustrate my predictions.

The main point emphasized in that letter was that

the aggressive group then in power in Japan would steadily push their country's expansion, and that they would not stop until they met a force superior in strength to their own. There was mentioned the fact that the Naval authorities wished to see Japan expand through the islands of the Pacific while the Army were only interested in expansion on the mainland of Asia. I wrote that since the Army was in control of the government naturally their plan would be followed. That if one would place before him a map of the Far East and put one leg of a divider on Tokyo and draw an arc of a circle with a radius of 1,500 miles from the Yangtze River on the south to the Sea of Okhotsk on the north he would see a sector of a circle which in my opinion would represent closely the ambition of the Japanese Army leaders *at that time*. I pointed out that Japan had always considered Vladivostok to be a dagger pointed at the heart of Japan; that Japan could easily cut the one Russian railway north of Manchuria and then take over all of Siberia to the east thereof including northern Saghalin; that I believed she was not planning to go south of the Yangtze because that would surely involve her with the British Empire, which I thought she would at that time prefer to avoid.

In that same letter or in one a little later I insisted strongly that the wisest course for the United States to take would be to draw a line on the map of the Far East and notify Japan that if she overstepped that line we would fight. I argued that sooner or later we would have to stop her so the sooner it was done, the better for all. Captain Cranford, my assistant, disagreed with me in this matter. He argued that the farther we let Japan expand the weaker she would be when we finally came to grips with her. My reply to that was that the farther she went the more military supplies and general resources she would have available to her. Well, anyway I sent in that effort of mine, and I have reason to believe that it received serious consideration not only at that time but that about 1938 it was dug out of the files and used by the head of the War Plans Division to strengthen his plan to increase our defensive forces in the region of the Philippines.

Our Last Grand Maneuvers

In November of 1931 we foreign Military Attachés were invited as usual to be guests of the Army at the big annual fall maneuvers. This time they were held in the most southern island, Kyushu. Everything was conducted about as before at such maneuvers except that there was noticeable something in the air that caused a little cooling in the association of the Japanese officers and us foreign officers. For instance, it was the first time we had not received some personal gift to commemorate the occasion. While there, a bombshell was thrown into our foreign group by the news that the Japanese Army in Manchuria had invited all the Military Attachés to be their guests on a tour of Manchuria. The other Military Attachés soon accepted but I was informed that my government did not look with favor on the idea.

In returning from these maneuvers, a two-day train ride, one of the first class sleepers was occupied entirely by Japanese and foreign officers.

After leaving Osaka, a suspicious thing happened. Suddenly I realized that there was no one in the car except the tall handsome Russian Military Attaché and myself. Then I recalled that upon leaving Osaka there were few others in the car and that unnoticed by me the few remaining Japanese officers had withdrawn from time to time. Of course, I suspected a setup of some kind. I suspected that they wanted us to get together and talk and that in preparation for such a possibility they probably had installed several dictographs in the car. There came to my mind then the various times during that fall when at big official dinners in Tokyo I found myself sitting next to the Russian Ambassador or one of his secretaries. You see at that time we had not yet officially recognized the Soviet regime and as officials of our government we were expected not to have any social intercourse with the officials of the Soviet government. So I suspected that the Japanese Intelligence had placed a dictography under the table near my seat.

During that fall since the incident at Mukden on September 18th, the Japanese had been slowly pushing the Russian control out of northern Manchuria, and this with very little opposition from the Russians. The Japanese had been moving so slowly that it looked like they might be afraid of some sort of a trap. They probably hoped we might say something to each other that would be a help to them. If so, they were disappointed for I did not converse with any of those Russians.

Now in this car they had again put us together. I did want to talk to that Russian Colonel but I was afraid of the dictographs. Finally, we did get together and while walking back and forth in the center of the car we had an interesting conversation. Finally, I got out the $64 question, "When are you going to stop letting the Japanese push you northward in Manchuria?" His answer was, "When we reach the Siberian border we will stop." And if you know your Far Eastern history you will remember that they did stop at the border of Siberia and Mongolia. In fact, the Japanese Army kept trying out the Russians along the Siberian and Mongolian borders for years after but always the Russians counterattacked in force regaining their border. Several years later, I learned that this Colonel was liquidated after his return to Moscow. That also happened to his successor at Tokyo. Certainly it has always been a very dangerous job being a diplomat for the Soviet government.

Of course, as soon as I arrived at my office in Tokyo I sent off a cable in code telling my government what the Russian Military Attaché had told me.

XVII

With the Japanese Army in Manchuria

Shortly after my return to Tokyo from the Imperial Maneuvers I was informed that our War Department had changed its mind, so I left within a few days with the other Military Attachés for Manchuria. It was to be a specially conducted tour with a little but bright young Intelligence Officer of the Japanese General Staff as our guide. So began one of the most interesting experiences of my life.

On the day we Military Attachés started for Manchuria the Chief of the Japanese General Staff gave out to the papers, both Japanese and foreign, a story that the foreign nations had requested permission for their Military Attachés to visit Manchuria. Of course, it was wholly contrary to the facts but I suppose that story was expected to please the Japanese people better than a statement that they, the Japanese, had invited us to go.

As I have said, at this time, the Japanese were slowly but surely taking over all of Manchuria. There was practically no resistance from the Russians and little effective resistance from the Chinese. The Japanese had already taken over Changchun, which was the junction point for the Japanese and the Russian controlled railway lines running from Port Arthur and Harbin. The Japanese had extended their conquest to the east along the railway from Changchun and again westward over the railway as far to the northwest as Tsitsihar. The city of Harbin and the main Siberian rail line east of Tsitsihar to Vladivostok was still under the control of the Russians as was all the country to the north of that line.

Foreign governments, especially the United States, were severely criticizing Japan for this aggression. Japan was then trying to sell the world the false idea that it was all the fault of the Chinese, who they claimed had started the rumpus by attacking the railway north of Mukden and removing the rails with intent to wreck the evening southbound express. I suppose that some high ranking officer in the Japanese Tokyo headquarters thought it advisable to get us Military Attachés over there and win us over to their side.

Arriving at Mukden, we were promptly shown the "exact spot" on the railway north of the city where they claimed the Chinese troops had placed a bomb and blown up a portion of the track. That night I had a long talk with a Major Hamada in my own hotel room. I knew that he was the General Staff Officer who in Mukden on that night of September 18-19th had handled the operations of the Japanese Army in their start to take over Manchuria. It was quite evident that he was most proud of the efficient part he had taken in that night's successful action against the Chinese troops near Mukden. To help along the conversation, I appeared to be much impressed by his interesting experience. After a number of stiff drinks he did a lot of bragging and practically admitted the falsity of their claim that the Chinese had blown up their railway.

At Changchun north of Mukden we were shown the battlefield nearby in which the Chinese were defeated and driven away. There and often later we were told by our hosts that in fighting the Chinese they always surrounded them on three sides but left one side open by which it would appear that they could escape. But they always arranged troops in ambush near the road leading from the open side so that they could slaughter the Chinese trying to escape. The Japanese would often say to us, "You know if you surround the Chinese they will fight, just like a rat cornered, and then you will lose a lot of men."

I recall at Changchun the Russian droskys, the dignified old Russian built hotel with its big rooms and high ceilings, and the Chinese boy behind the hotel bar who talked rather freely that evening to us but was not there the next morning or that next evening.

Our next stop was the city of Kirin, east of Changchun. Here we were shown large numbers of Chinese troops that had been organized by the Japanese to help keep order in Manchuria. They did not impress me favorably and we doubted their dependability. Upon returning to Changchun, we were told that we would have the privilege of interviewing the Prime Minister of "Manchukuo," a Chinese puppet whom the Japanese had set up to help them in their claim that Manchukuo or Manchuria had become an independent nation. At first we were inclined to decline the privilege but thought better of it and soon found our group in his presence. As we had anticipated, he sat in a big chair with Japanese advisors standing one on each side and one in the rear. The Japanese wanted us to ask questions. We did put one or two, but seeing that his replies were prompted by his Japanese advisors we declined to ask more. What the Japanese thought they would accomplish by that little sideshow is not clear. Maybe they used it for propaganda throughout the world. I never checked that possibility.

Our next move from Changchun was to the north to Harbin. At this time the Japanese had not yet taken over Harbin. Russians and Chinese were still running the Chinese Eastern Railway which runs east and west through Harbin and also southward to Changchun. As we rode northward by rail, I was in a large compartment with the British Military Attaché. I recall some Chinese officials, Customs Officers I suppose, came to our compartment and asked to see our baggage, which was piled up on the racks above our heads. I started to get mine down but the Britisher said, "Damned if I get mine down." They were quite insistent but then the Britisher said, "You speak to the Japanese Officer who is in charge of us." Like a flash their attitude changed and they left not to return.

It was so evident everywhere how greatly the Chinese attitude toward foreigners and especially toward the Japanese, had changed in the past year. One year before they had been quite confident and even cocky toward the Japanese. Now they were scared and even servile. It has been claimed that the Chinese Manchurian chief, Chang Hsueh Idang, had given orders for no resistance. Evidently he planned to depend on the League of Nations.

It was during these days that our Secretary of War Stimson was sending so many strong notes to Japan. He had the Japanese fighting mad most of the time. But they were really not ready for war with us. Was Stimson willing that war come then? Perhaps it would have been best, but I understood at the time that the British would not go along with us in risking war. The British Military Attaché argued with me that the taking over of all Manchuria would satisfy the Japanese and keep them busy for a long time. Japan's success in her aggressive moves in

Manchuria encouraged Mussolini and Mussolini's success encouraged Hitler. It is possible that had we stopped Japan at once, World War II would not have been necessary.

At Harbin we were introduced to some pro-Japanese Chinese who we supposed would take charge at Harbin when the Japanese decided to oust the White Russians. While in this city, we were given a Japanese dinner with a noted geisha present to help entertain us.

Returning to Changhung we passed to the south spending the night in a Japanese inn at Tsupinkai. The next morning we boarded a special train for the west passing through Taonan to the battlefields to the north toward Tsitsihar. It was on those fields that the Japanese forces suffered so severely from the cold. When we were in the Mukden station we had seen the results of the cold—men lying all over the floor with bandaged feet and hands. Their winter uniform had not arrived in time for their soldiers before they were ordered into that campaign.

Throughout this month we were fed royally. One meal would be Chinese, the next Japanese, then Russian, French, English—all sorts—and the best that could be obtained—with wines and liqueurs appropriate to each type of meal. In our small car on the rear of the special train on the battlefield south of Tsitsihar our big table was covered at luncheon time with all sorts of good cold food. A really fine meal which surprised us and we ate heartily after our long walk over the battlefield. But imagine our surprise when we found that it was only the beginning—the hors d'oeuvre course of a big Russian meal. Of course, we were able to do little more than taste the delicious hot courses that followed.

Late that afternoon we arrived in Tsitsihar, which

we found to be a large Chinese city with almost no foreign-style buildings. Most of the store fronts were boarded up. That night we had a fine beef steak meal in a Russian restaurant. After finishing our repast we were called to a serious conference in which we were told that Chinese "bandits" were operating on the railway to the south over which we had that afternoon arrived in Tsitsihar. They asked us whether we wished to remain in Tsitsihar that night or run the risk of the bandits and go south to the crossing of the main east-west railway and spend the night at the little hotel there as originally planned. Naturally, we could not tell whether they were giving us the real facts or not. It might have been staged to impress us. Finally, we decided to go. Our special train moved without lights under heavy guard of Japanese soldiers. Nothing unusual happened.

That night we slept as planned in the small hotel at the railway junction south of Tsitsihar. It was a strange place—a two-story foreign style building of white stucco exterior with long narrow halls, small rooms, each heated by a separate large stove whose door opened into the hall so that the Chinese janitor could tend to it without coming into the room. Big Chinese guards slept on the floor outside our doors that night. No doubt we were guarded throughout our journey in Manchuria by plainclothesmen. The Japanese, of course, would not want anything serious to happen to any one of us.

At breakfast the next morning we had excellent bread, butter, ham, and tea in glasses in the ten by fifteen-foot dining room. The bread and butter made a hit with me as it was really superior, something I had not seen since leaving the United States.

During all this trip I had been wearing the Japanese Officers' winter fur uniform. It was necessary to keep me from suffering in that climate. Of course, I had removed all insignia. It was much more efficient for protection from the cold than any uniform I had seen in our Army. Naturally, I later sent a detailed description of it to the War Department.

Leaving that little hotel at the railway junction south of Tsitsihar we headed for Harbin over the Chinese Eastern Railway. All of that part of Manchuria in the fall is flat and barren in appearance—much like a desert. Of course, this is not true of the southeastern part of Manchuria, which has much forest land and is hilly, if not mountainous, in spots. Near the railway stations west of Harbin were immense piles of soya beans in sacks. They were not covered over or protected in any way. But I was told that there is no rain or snow in those parts at that time of year. I suppose those beans were waiting for sufficient rolling stock to move them—to where I do not know, but suspect to the south for the Japanese to use in various ways.

At that time there were practically no soya beans raised in America. It is hard to understand why we were so slow in learning of the possibilities of that grain. I like to think that I had a small part in introducing it to our country for whenever I went to my old home on a farm in Ohio I often spoke about the great quantities of the bean I had seen in China and of the many uses the Japanese were finding for it. My brother, who was a very progressive farmer, later became the president of the Soya Bean Association of the United States.

This time we did not stop at Harbin but transferred at once to the road running south to Mukden.

About this time I had to go on the water wagon and be careful of what I ate. The variety and quantity of rich food and alcoholics had evidently upset the lining of my stomach.

During all this time in Manchuria the Chinese and Japanese armies were fighting each other. Every day we would be furnished a copy of the Intelligence Report of the Japanese Army. It was quite evident that through these reports the Japanese were trying to convince us that it was really the Chinese Army that was on the offensive and that naturally the Japanese had to protect themselves.

Of course, I had none of my official codes with me. I had, however, arranged a private code with my assistant left in charge of the office in Tokyo. That one I knew could be used but once for it soon could be broken. So what I did was to send in the clear, that is in plain English, uncoded, to the Tokyo office, telegrams in which I would state, "Japanese Army Intelligence states." Then would follow quotations of extracts of any parts of the reports furnished to me which I thought might be of interest to Tokyo and Washington. I never added any opinion of my own. This seemed to please the Japanese, and why not, were they not getting their ideas into Washington unchanged? The sad part came for me later when I learned that the State Department had thought that I believed those extracts from the Japanese reports.

From our travels in North Manchuria we returned to Mukden and there prepared to join the Japanese Army just starting out on a drive southwest along the Mukden-Peking railway toward Chinchow. All over Manchuria we had seen Japanese soldiers moving here and there but now we had actually joined a large force as they moved forth for battle. Starting in the morning, by noon we were near the front line. It was possible for us to reach the front so quickly because we had been provided a special train.

At this time an unusual thing happened. Our train had been placed on a side track and we were wondering if we would go forward from there by walking. Suddenly, we saw a troop train filled with Japanese soldiers moving to the rear on the main line. Some of the cars had large field guns aboard. Evidently the Japanese Army was retiring. But why? It could not be that they had been defeated. No such opposition had yet been found in Manchuria. We strongly suspected that some order halting their advance must have come from the Emperor in person. And now I understand that is just what happened. It appears that a strong note from the President of the United States had caused this unheard of action of the Emperor. Perhaps the first time in Japanese history.

Later our own train backed up and returned to Mukden. Here we were swamped with Japanese intelligence reports indicating that the Chinese had many divisions advancing along that Peking-Mukden railway for the purpose of attacking Mukden. Much of this I sent to the Tokyo Embassy as before, stating, "The Japanese intelligence states." This although, I felt sure that any troops the Chinese had on that railway were without doubt for the purpose of hindering and delaying any movement of the Japanese Army toward the southwest. Their mission would be entirely a defensive one.

Just about one month after we started on that trip through Manchuria we were assembled in Mukden and told that our visit was now ended; that we were no longer their guests so we could now go as we pleased. Soon they asked each of us what we planned to do. All except me said that they would return at once to Tokyo. My answer was that I did not yet know what I would do.

Upon returning to my hotel there was a very timely telegram awaiting me. It was in the private code of which I had spoken before. Hurrying to my room, I eagerly decoded it and found that it authorized my going on into northern China if I so desired. At once, I went to the room of the big Scotsman who was the manager of that Mukden-Peking railway. I asked him if it was safe for me to go through on his regular passenger train to North China. He assured me that it was safe. So I decided to go but told no one.

XVIII
With the Chinese Army

The morning following our dismissal by our Japanese hosts I was in the hotel lobby bright and early, but not too early for our little Japanese General Staff officer guide. He was there and came up at once to inquire as to my plans. I replied, "I am taking the early train for Tientsin." He then said, "But that is unwise for there is much danger from bandits." I replied, "I am not alarmed about that because the manager of the railway has told me that it is quite safe." That last remark of mine was a mistake. I should not have mentioned the big Scotsman as you will see later.

Well, I chased across town in a rikasha and made the train. In my car were a number of Japanese, one of whom spoke good English and insisted on conversing with me. Undoubtedly, he was an intelligence agent. When we arrived at the end of the area patrolled by the Japanese soldiers, all the Japanese vacated the car and I was left wholly alone to traverse no-man's-land for a few miles. Then in came some Chinese, one of whom could speak good English. He welcomed me and told me that most of the Military Attachés to China, including the American, were now living at Chinchow, about half way from Mukden to Shanhaikwan. He suggested that I stop off there, which I readily consented to do.

At Chinchow I found Lieutenant Colonel Margetts, our Military Attaché to China, and several others all living in a large foreign-style school building that was surrounded by a high stone wall. They appeared to look on me as a strange animal from a hostile world. I found that my cables had been repeated to Margetts. The Military Attachés at Chinchow had been sending reports to their home governments, which did not agree with mine at all, from Manchuria. Remember mine had been largely quotations from the Japanese Intelligence reports. They were very anxious to show me that my reports had contained misleading information. And, of course, I was most willing to be shown.

That evening I had a long talk with Margetts as we strolled about the walled compound out of hearing of any little pitchers with big ears. At dinner and later, Margetts introduced me to the other Military Attachés including the big German who was there but very quiet and unobtrusive, sitting at a table by himself.

The following morning I was taken to the headquarters of the Commanding General of all the Chinese Forces operating between the Great Wall and Mukden. This headquarters was in small Chinese houses not far away. An American would call them stone huts. There I was shown the big map of the general military situation. On it were the positions marked of the Chinese Divisions and even smaller units down to and including battalions at the front. They said that they would like to have me check the position of their troops in any way I might wish.

You see the Japanese Intelligence had claimed that the Chinese divisions in large numbers were moving to attack Mukden and that this forced them to take aggressive action from Mukden toward Chinchow. On the other hand, the Chinese were claiming before the League at

201

Geneva that they were entirely passive, only trying to defend themselves when attacked by the Japanese. I already believed what the Chinese claimed but I had not yet seen for myself.

After a study of the map it was evident that the claims of the Japanese were very incorrect and misleading if the map was correct. Numbered divisions were not shown where the Japanese had reported them and several divisions, which the Japanese had reported moving on Mukden were not shown there but way back as Reserves in north China near Tientsin and Peking. I suspected that the Chinese map was correct, but I did not act as though I were convinced as to its correctness.

The Chinese General suggested that I check the accuracy of the map. He said that every facility for travel was at my disposal. So then I took down the number and location of several of the smaller units in a notebook. I showed no one what I had written. They took me to a special train. All the other Military Attachés came along but kept in the background with little to say. The train commander asked me, "Where does the Colonel wish to go?" I named the station near one of the units I had entered in my notebook. The train then pulled out and we all traveled to that point. Upon arrival there the train commander then asked, "And now, where?" I replied, "To the town of ———." In a short time there came a funny old carriage with ponies hitched to it. So off I went with Colonel Margetts and a Staff Officer of the Chinese forces. As we rode over the country we were guarded by a troop of Chinese Cavalry riding before and behind us. A movie of my activities on that day would have been both amusing and interesting.

Upon arrival at the Chinese town the Chinese officer asked, "And now what?" I replied, "Take me to the headquarters of the ——th Regiment." This, they soon did. There I was told about the disposition of the entire regiment. They said that two of the battalions were out on frontline duty and a third was in reserve nearby. The exact positions of the two frontline battalions was given me. I noticed this disposition agreed with the map at General Headquarters from which I had taken my notes. I then said, "Have the Reserve Battalion paraded for me." In a very brief time they took me to a field nearby where I saw the companies of the battalion assembling. I personally looked at individual men, checking their insignia, and inquiring through an interpreter as to their battalion number, company letter, billets, etc.

"Now, where Colonel?" "Back to the train." "Now where?" "Go to ——— over on this branch line," indicating on our map. This sort of thing was repeated four or five times enough to convince me that the big Situation Map I had studied that morning was correct. Near the end of the day I requested that the train return to Chinchow.

I had said nothing to indicate that I was learning so I could see that both the foreigners and Chinese were very eager to hear something from me. As soon as we had returned to the school building, I went into Colonel Margetts' room. He had the large War Department code book. I suspected that the Japanese would have a copy of it by that time but it was all we had so I wrote a cable in longhand to go to the War Department in Washington just as soon as Margetts' office force could encode it, something like the following, "I have this day carefully checked in person the actual positions of the Chinese troops between Shanhaikwan and Mukden and am convinced that the recent claims of the Japanese Intelligence concerning Chinese troops in this area are almost wholly false."

When Colonel Margetts told the other Military Attachés about the contents of my cable there was much rejoicing. I was quite the popular kid about town. Not such a Japanophile as they had thought. Later I heard that my cable had caused quite a sensation in Washington and that Secretary of State Stimson had said that it was much to Colonel McIlroy's credit that he should admit that he was wrong in his previous reports. Ye Gods! I did not change my mind. I had not once said in any of my cables from Manchuria to the Embassy in Tokyo that I believed so and so. I had kept repeating "The Japanese Intelligence reports." It would be interesting to look through the old files to see if and when that expression had been *eliminated* from my reports. I think that it would be found to have still been in the copy handed the State Department. It is my guess that they simply misinterpreted it.

XIX
In North China Again

On the day following my unusual experience with the Chinese Army in Manchuria I left by rail for Tientsin. On the way I continued to check the locations of Chinese divisions by getting off at stations and observing the troops which would usually be there to meet someone or to secure supplies.

At Tientsin I stopped with my sister and Lieutenant Colonel Walter S. Drysdale. The latter was still the Executive of the 15th Infantry, which was stationed in Tientsin. The Commanding Officer of the Regiment had me lecture to the officers of his Regiment on my observations in Manchuria. After a few days in Tientsin I accompanied my sister and her husband to Peking. In Peking we stopped, this time, at a foreign hotel. During the few days I was in that city I made a few necessary official calls on our Legation officials and attended some interesting luncheons and dinners.

I was amazed at the apparent general indifference of American diplomats in that city toward me and what I could tell them. I knew of course, from past association, that our entire State Department was sold lock, stock, and barrel on China and the Chinese. I think they thought that I was very pro-Japanese and could have nothing of interest for them. We experts on Japan had often had reason to resent the attitude of the State Department toward us. The Chinese experts always seemed to get the breaks from Washington. We had no more liking for the Japanese Army group which believed it their duty to see that Japan ruled the world than did the diplomatic and military group of our country who were so pro-Chinese. But we did realize that there were fine people in Japan just as in every other country and in all races of people. No doubt the representatives of the west coast in Washington had their influence in this matter. I recall one evening in 1934 in Virginia at a private dinner party a woman from California said to my wife and me across the table, "Now, honestly did you ever see one good side to the character of the Japanese?" We tried to answer her quietly and tactfully along the line that there is always something good in everyone and that in all countries one could discover fine people. Suddenly she flared up and said, "I wish their islands would sink into the ocean until not even the tip of Fuji could be seen." Naturally that ended that conversation.

The most intelligent questioner with whom I talked while in Peking on this visit was the seventy-odd-year-old wife of our retired General Crozier. Mrs. Crozier was one of the guests at a luncheon given by the First Secretary of the Embassy I believe. She got me off in a corner and shot one searching question after another at me. I suspected that she would report my replies to the Embassy or Washington.

One day while in Peking I dropped over to see the train from Mukden come in. You may recall my stating that I had made a mistake in telling the Japanese Intelligence officer that the manager of the Peking-Mukden railway had told me that it was quite safe to travel on that road. Well, here is the proof of my mistake. As I stood there watching the train pull into the station I suddenly realized that the train must have been attacked by bandits for there were many marks of bullets on the side of the cars and several broken windows. Later, I corroborated my belief from the passengers that they had been attacked and robbed on their way down—and one of the passengers was—yes, that very manager who had been so rash as to tell me it was safe. We can hardly consider that a coincidence. Now the statement of the Japanese officer to me that the road was unsafe had been proved to have been correct, and the manager would probably be careful in the future about advising Military Attachés to travel over it.

My return to Tokyo about the end of December was made by sea. A hearty welcome awaited me from my family. But it was a cold reception I received from my acquaintances in the Japanese War Department and General Staff. When I met them at various places they avoided seeing me when possible, only speaking when really forced to. One day Colonel Watari, the Assistant to the Minister of War, cornered me in the hall of the War Department building and in a most indignant manner asked, "Why did you tell your War Department that our Intelligence reports in Manchuria were false?" I replied, "Because I found out they were incorrect." He said, "Now listen, it would be alright for you to tell civilians such things but you should not expect trained Army officers to believe them." My reply was, "I think too much of your intelligence to believe that last statement." He walked away without another word.

XX

Tokyo, January to July, 1932

Early in 1931 we had been fortunate in obtaining a high-class home in Takanawa in the southern part of Tokyo not far from Shinagawa station. I have described it in Chapter XII, page 111.

When a Military Attaché must have his office in his own house it is difficult if not impossible to keep any secrets from other nations. I had a large safe but knew from experience in running the Far Eastern Section of the Military Intelligence Division in Washington that secrets in such a safe could not remain long away from any nation interested enough to be willing to pay the price for them. Besides I had reason to believe that the Japanese Army had its own code breaking department. A number of times I spent the late hours after returning from some official dinner in getting out in code all by myself a lengthy cablegram to the War Department, only to learn a few days later that the Japanese General Staff knew what I had sent. They must have broken my code or else there was a leak in the government in Washington, both are quite possible.

As I have said before, life was quite exciting and strenuous for me in Tokyo from the time of the Mukden incident until I left for the United States in March 1933. I considered it my main duty to keep Washington informed on the Japanese troops, that is on mobilization, movement of units to Manchuria, new weapons, and the rate of manufacturing airplanes, tanks, etc.

Soon after returning from Manchuria I subscribed to a large number of local papers from various sections of Japan and hired a few Japanese translators to scan them and give me in English that which I was interested in. To check the translators I had some of my student officers look over a few of the papers after they had been gone over by the translators to see if they had failed to note the articles in which I was interested. It was surprising how much information we secured that way for about three weeks. There would be the mention of some soldier home on furlough from such a unit in such a place. The account of a send-off for some conscript or reservist going to such a unit at such place. I would place those clippings, many of them on the top of my desk and spend hours shuffling them about until I found some important information they contained. It was like working out a Chinese puzzle. But of course, the Japanese Intelligence soon learned of this scheme and no doubt sent out orders all over the country to their local papers, for gradually the papers no longer contained those little bits of news useful to me. Then I cancelled my subscription to the papers, dismissed my translators, and looked for some other way of securing information.

Naturally, I made as many inspections of schools, arsenals, airfields, etc., as they would permit. They often said yes but would put all objects which they did not wish me to see out of sight and often there was a building or two into which they would not let us have a peek. But let me tell you how we outwitted them on one occasion. Information indicated that they were making a new tank at an arsenal in Omori, just south of Tokyo on the way to Yokohama. My request to visit that arsenal with my assistant was granted. We went and saw nothing of interest, only old models and the place was really not busy so we decided we were being cheated in a big way. After returning to our office, I told my assistant to take an early morning train for Yokohama the next morning and watch the roads in the vicinity of Omori for new weapons going back into the arsenal. He came back elated and saying that he had seen not only a new tank but a new type of military bus. He could give only a general description of the tank and bus but knowing they existed we told the language students and it was not long till we had more detailed information about them.

For some time I was anxious to know the location of the Heavy Bombing Regiment. Their permanent station was at Hamamatsu on the coast north of Nagoya. If they had been sent to Manchuria it would mean that serious operations had been planned for the near future over there. Twice I asked permission to visit Hamamatsu and twice I was refused. But then not long after a funny thing happened. They had given permission for me to visit a new arsenal, not yet in operation, near Shimonoseki in Kyushu. The Commanding Officer, who had been in charge of its construction, had studied arsenals in the United States for a long time. Strange to say, he apparently was very pro-American. He treated me very well. I told him about my plans for my return trip to Tokyo how I was going first to the hot springs at Beppu on the southern shore of the Inland Sea, thence by boat to Osaka, and then by air to Tokyo. Incidentally, I had wired my family the hour of my expected arrival at the Tokyo airport. Skipping over other experiences on this trip, we will jump to when I found myself in a four passenger plane flying over the rice paddies and bays along the shore of east cen-

210

tral Japan going north from Osaka to Tokyo. Suddenly I realized we were losing altitude rapidly. It alarmed me for I knew there was no scheduled stop between Osaka and Tokyo. Soon we landed on a large flat field, quite evidently an air field. We were told by the pilot that the engine had not been performing well and that it would be sometime before they would take off again. As I had noticed nothing unusual about the action of the engine, it made me suspicious. As I looked about the field and saw the large hangars I realized this was the heavy bomber field at Hamamatsu which I had asked twice to inspect. Now what to do? Why had this stop been made here? Had one of my acquaintances in the Japanese Intelligence Division decided that it would be advisable to let me see the place. Or had they laid some trap for me, hoping that in my eagerness to learn all I could I would overstep and give them a club over my head. This was not the first time they had tried to place me in an embarrassing position. So far I had escaped. So I personally talked to the pilot expressing my disappointment at the delay. Then, casually, I took a long look around studying the lay of the land and the type and position of all the buildings in sight. Then I lay down on the warm grass in the sun as the other passengers had done. Finally, I decided to go further for I thought they would not search me. I rolled over on my tummy and pulling out the map of our route, began a rough drawing of the airfield. The important information I obtained was that the Bombing Regiment was no longer there. The place was dead, the hangars empty. This, I reported as soon as possible after reaching home.

It was very necessary that I keep Washington well informed as possible concerning the Japanese Air Force. This was difficult, especially for an Infantryman as I was. For a long time, I had urged Washington to send me even for a short time, an air officer as one of my assistants. Several times I was refused. The reason given for the refusal was that since the air officer would not be able to take his official flights, he would not be able to draw his flying pay to which he was accustomed. Strange that a thing like that would interfere. My assistants and language students had no flying pay and they expected to go wherever ordered.

But at last relief did come. From the Philippines came a Major Duty. I believe he was an air officer of the Philippine Scouts or of the Philippine Army. He claimed he was on a three-week leave of absence. His attractive wife and daughter came with him. Within a few days after he had settled in Tokyo he called at my office and told me that he would be glad to help me in any way possible while he was there on leave. Naturally, I welcomed his help and soon had him busy. Before he left, we had prepared together a complete revision of the write up on the Japanese Air Force and sent it off for file in Washington. His expert knowledge as an Air Officer and my experience in what was wanted and how it should be prepared enabled us to produce something of which we were both proud. Very promptly I had a letter from Washington complimenting us on the excellence of those reports. The letter said that they had felt the lack of good information on the subject and were more than pleased to receive something even better than they had expected to get. I never tried to find out for sure but I always suspected that Major Duty's flying pay was made up in some way through some other Intelligence funds available to General MacArthur or from money provided by the Philippine government.

Let me tell you here how I had to go about getting information on the Japanese Air Force. The Japanese authorities would not permit me to visit their airplane factories. Our government wanted to know as much as possible about how many planes of each type the Japanese Army was making and could make, say in a year's time. One of their fighters was made right in Tokyo and yet we knew little about its rate of production. From my assistant, Captain Cranford, I learned that there was a Swedish businessman who sold ball bearings in great quantity to the Japanese government. Further inquires brought out that he was married to an American woman, that he liked to associate with Americans, and that he liked to impress people with his importance. I soon managed to make his acquaintance and before long invited him to the American Club for luncheon. There I brought the conversation around to his career. He was soon telling me with evident real pleasure about his rapid rise to a fine position in his own company. This led naturally to his remarkable success with orders in Japan. Before long, he had mentioned a large sale of bearings to the Tokyo fighter plane factory. He told me that those bearings could be used for propellers only. He told me the exact quantity ordered, when the first consignment must be delivered, and when the last delivery must be made. That was almost too easy. I continued to cultivate my acquaintance with him. He was a likable fellow. But soon he told me that he had displeased the Japanese Army officers very much by his association with me so I had to let him alone after that. Being crafty or sharp in my dealings with my associates was most distasteful to me. My nature was naturally frank and open. Just a grown up boy off a farm in Union County, Ohio. But in such a position, I felt that it was up to me to use any method possible, almost, to secure the important information my government needed.

213

Here is an example of how I secured background needed in my search for military information. Mr. Neville, as Counselor of the Embassy, was my immediate superior. Like most diplomats he was very closemouthed. Too much so I thought toward me. It was a habit with him and generally speaking it is a good trait in a diplomat. Everything I learned was passed on to him. From him I needed background to keep me from going on the wrong track and often doing much unnecessary work. He just would not cooperate. So I persuaded him to come out to my house now and then to play tennis with me. Following the tennis, we would have a good shower and then a long drink or two of what he liked best. By that time, his reserve was down and often he would open up and really chat with me laughing over his various troubles. In this way I picked up that which I considered was rightfully mine anyway. That information was a great help.

Permit me to quote here from *The Far Eastern Crisis* written by Henry L. Stimson, our Secretary of State during the Manchurian trouble. "As a matter of fact throughout this crisis in Manchuria of which I am writing, the American government was served so efficiently by its agents and representatives on the ground that we were habitually placed in the position of having in our hands earlier and more accurate information than almost any other country." I hope and believe that my office in Tokyo was no small part of the source of his correct information during that trying period.

The Shanghai Affair

In January of 1932, a new and serious situation developed in the Far East. This time in Shanghai. The Japanese Navy had been quite jealous of the Army because of the latter's successful activity in behalf of their country on the mainland of Asia. They were also anxious to become heroes in the eyes of their countrymen. So when trouble occurred in Shanghai, they promptly took it as an excuse to land their sailors there. But they found that the Chinese troops in that city were quite different in their fighting ability to those in Manchuria. They fought back with bravery and ability, so much so that the sailors could not handle the situation. The Japanese Army had not approved of the Navy's going into that city and so were much displeased when they had to go into that hot spot to save the situation for Japan. Even the Army found it very difficult to make headway against those exceptional Chinese troops, and soon realized that a large operation would be necessary to clear up the situation for them.

When the Shanghai affair broke I tried to secure permission to go there to observe. I was anxious to see any new equipment or methods of fighting they might find it necessary to use. The State Department said, "No." Then I tried to have them let one or two of my student officers go. Again, "No." No explanation was ever given my office for this refusal. They did permit our Military Attaché to China, his student officers, and many young officers on leave from Manila to go there. But we experts on the Japanese Army, who spoke their language, were not permitted to go. I have never been able to understand that attitude of the State Department. The result was that the War Department received little information of any value at that time, and I believe that much of value could have been learned by an expert. Some time later, I was swamped by copies of long detailed reports made by young officers on leave passing through Shanghai, sent on to me from the War Department for me to study and extract therefrom the material for the Japanese digest in the Military Intelligence Division files in Washington. In all those reports there was not one useful new thing worth putting in the digest.

Immediately after the Shanghai affair broke, the Italian Military Attaché went down there. I kept in touch with his Embassy and as soon as he returned I went over to have tea with him. He was full of his interesting experience and eager to tell them to an interested understanding listener. He laughed about the Americans he had seen there. Said they would stop and spend much time studying matters and equipment old as the Japanese Army itself while he passed on to observe something new and worthwhile observing. From him I did get a few new facts and ideas about the Japanese Army and that is all we did get out of Shanghai that winter. All the effort of our officers was wasted except that some of our officers had had the opportunity to observe Japanese troops.

During the winter of 1931-32 the new Embassy buildings were completed. Our Ambassador, Mr. Forbes, moved into his new home on the hill overlooking the big office building and two apartment structures. I was given three large rooms extending across the eastern end of the first floor. The Naval Attaché had one room I believe off the hall leading to my office and I believe that is all he needed under his simple efficient set up.

Mr. Forbes' brother's wife and daughter soon joined him in his superb new home to help him socially. The Forbes were all fine people.

Ever since the Mukden incident in September 1931, our Secretary of State had been sending very strong notes to the Japanese government. Those sharp notes angered the Japanese authorities, especially the Army group that was in actual control. The situation grew worse as the winter wore along. Our Ambassador began to have frequent meetings at night in the library of his new residence. Present at those secret conferences would be the Counselor, Mr. Neville, the Naval Attaché, Captain Johnston and I. After a round of good Irish whiskey from the Ambassador's barrel, the situation would be presented to us orally by the Ambassador, after which each of us was encouraged to express himself. After a full discussion, Mr. Forbes would dictate to his confidential man "Friday" and we would soon have a proposed cable to the Secretary of State about the then situation for criticism. Those meetings were very interesting. It was then that Mr. Forbes' evident executive ability best showed itself.

The situation gradually became very serious. I have always suspected that Mr. Stimson was willing that our country go to war to stop Japan provided he had the support of the British. And I am inclined to believe that a war then might have been won with comparative ease and perhaps a World War II avoided. I recall being at an informal family tea at the British Embassy one afternoon when the British Ambassador took me to one side and told me that he had insisted with his Home Office that England not go to war with the Japanese until the Singapore defenses were completed.

Another time our Ambassador called in his Counselor, and the Military, Naval, and Commercial Attachés and asked us if anyone had a secret code that we believed had not been broken already by the Japanese. He told us he had a cable to send Mr. Stimson that would warn him that the Japanese were about to go to war with us. To my surprise, no one offered a code although we each had several. Previously I had reported my codes under suspicion and I suppose the others had. So Mr. Forbes sent his important message in a private code of his own, by the Cap-

217

tain of an American liner from Yokohama to Shanghai and from there by cable. Shortly after, I received a cable ordering me to explain why I had told my Ambassador that I had no safe code. It was easily explained and nothing more was heard on that subject. We had a special code section in our Military Intelligence Division but I had long felt that it was either inefficient or had too few personnel to do its job properly.

And now I come to one of my most unusual experiences during my tour as a Military Attaché in Japan. One day our Ambassador summoned me to his residence. There I found Mr. Neville, our Counselor. Mr. Forbes appeared quite alarmed over the situation. He told us that Japan was about to go to war with us and that he wanted us both to do something to prevent a war. He said he wanted immediate action. He said that what we did would be on our own; that we must make it understood we were acting on our own initiative without orders. I asked one question, "Governor, what do you think Mr. Stimson wants? War or peace?" Mr. Forbes replied, "I do not know what he wants, but I do know what he would want—peace—and you will conduct yourselves accordingly."

Well, you can imagine my feelings as I left the Ambassador's residence and walked slowly back down to my fine large office in the new handsome office building on ground below the Ambassador's residence. At first, I had not the slightest idea as to what I was going to do to carry out the instructions of my superior, except being a well-disciplined product of West Point and twenty-eight years in the Army, I knew that I was going to do something and that something would be a real effort. Mr. Neville went his own way. We did not cooperate or compare notes. If anything like that was to be done I thought

218

it was up to Mr. Neville to make the suggestion as he was my immediate superior in the Embassy. I also realized that what he attempted to do would have little effect on the situation because he would be dealing with members of the Japanese Foreign Office which no longer had any power over international affairs. On the contrary, I would be dealing with the War Department in which the real power in Japan lay. My only idea as I returned to my office was to get hold of and study again my maps of the Shanghai situation, which was the immediate cause of the possibility of war.

Sitting at my desk I pulled out my maps of Shanghai and vicinity which I had personally marked up in colors to picture the military situation. After refreshing my memory from those maps, I rolled up the map of the general situation in Shanghai, tucked it under my arm and started for the War Department about a mile distant. When I left the office, I had no definite plan in mind. But as I walked slowly along a plan began to emerge from the jumble of ideas then in my mind. I would go to see Colonel Watari, the Secretary to the Minister of War. He spoke English well and knew the United States. I would have an earnest talk with him and perhaps between us we could work out something that might be acceptable to both our countries. But before I had reached the Japanese War Department compound, there had formed in my mind a definite proposition to put before Watari. So I entered the sacred precincts of the Japanese War Department with good morale.

Well, I found Watari promptly. He took me into one of their small foreign-style rooms kept especially for conferences. There we sat down at a table. There was none of the pleasant opening greetings and conversation such as we would have had before the Mukden incident. Almost at once I began what I suspect was one of, if not the best, speech I ever made. Thinking back over it afterwards, I was quite proud of myself. Of course, I was deeply stirred inside by the importance of what I was attempting to do. It was my first experience directly on the diplomatic firing line.

My line of talk was something like the following. It was expressed forcibly and with much feeling. "Watari, I am here on my own, as an individual not as a representative of my government. You know and I know that our countries are in great danger of going to war. I do not want war and I know you should not want war. It would be a terrible catastrophe for both countries. Your country has never been defeated in war but my country also has never been defeated in war. I tell you now if it does come to war, my country will give you an awful licking even if it should take three years to do it, and when we get through with you, you won't be a first-class power, you will be a fifth-rate power or even lower. As I see it, you and I have the opportunity of our lives right now, here, to do a wonderful service for our countries. Are you willing now to talk over with me the possibilities for a peaceful settlement of that Shanghai situation?"

You see I knew already from certain sources that the Japanese Army was sick of the troubles into which the Navy had drawn them in Shanghai. Watari's eyes flashed excitedly as I talked to him. He looked intensely interested. I also knew that the Army was terribly peeved because we had interfered so much in what they considered their right to expand in Manchuria. The League of Nations Commission that was sent to Japan was very irritating to their proud nationalism. Every note of Mr. Stimson was most provoking to them. I knew Watari no

220

longer felt kindly toward me. His eyes seemed to show hatred instead.

Watari's reply was, simply, "If you have a plan I will be glad to hear it." Then I drew out my map and there followed a discussion in which I outlined my idea for bringing about a peaceful settlement of the Shanghai situation and in so doing, avoiding a war between our countries. Generally, my plan was: The Japanese forces to withdraw from those parts of the city not included in the recognized Japanese sector. The American and British forces to move in and take over as the Japanese withdrew. No Chinese troops to be permitted in that portion evacuated by the Japanese forces. Finally, no Japanese Army or Navy forces to be left in Shanghai with the exception of local police in the Japanese sector. After we had talked the plan over, I again tried to impress him with the opportunity he now had to do something for his country. He had calmed down. His face looked quite different. It looked more friendly, and I would say more hopeful. He merely said, "I will present your idea to the Minister of War at once and will call you when I have something to tell you." It was late in the afternoon. I left at once for my home in the hills in the southern part of Tokyo. Gwynneth and I had a most important dinner scheduled for that evening. Nothing less than a dinner with the Crown Prince and Princess Chichibu at their unofficial home in the rear of the Crown Prince's big imposing palace.

I was somewhat worried for fear that the situation might develop so that it would clash with that dinner engagement. An invitation to the home of a member of the Imperial family was naturally an order. To arrive a little late even would be a bad error. I was hoping that nothing would happen to compel me to make a decision that would interfere with that important engagement. But, apparently, that is just what did happen. About 7:10 P.M., when Gwynneth and I were putting on our very best bib and tucker, our telephone rang. I took down the receiver of our bedroom extension. It was Colonel Watari asking me to come down to the War Department at once as he had something of importance to tell me. I replied that I would be down as soon as possible and hung up. Turning about I saw that Gwynneth was alarmed. She said, "What are you doing? You can't miss this dinner. We must not even be late." I said this was more important than the dinner, my lateness or absence could be explained later.

I immediately called a servant and ordered a taxi to come in all haste. As I finished dressing in my white tie and long-tailed civilian formal evening dress, I told Gwynneth to follow me in our car to the War Department and wait outside the building for me as long as she could and still make the dinner on time. Then I grabbed my tall silk hat and off I went as fast as the chauffeur could drive safely.

Arriving at the gate of the wall surrounding the War Department buildings I found it closed and locked. It was now dark, about 7:45 P.M. And we were due at the Crown Prince's home at 8:00 o'clock. Without hesitation I told the taxi driver to drive up close to the wall. Then I stood on the front fender and from there managed to draw myself up to the top of the stone wall. Fortunately, there was no broken glass on top as was quite common in Japan. I peered down into the dark interior looking for a possible sentry for I did not relish the idea of having a bayonet shoved into me. Seeing no sentry, I dropped down on the inside little the worse for my unusual entry. I hurried to the War Department building. There I found a light in the main hall and a soldier at the entrance who at once conducted me to the same little conference room on the second floor where Colonel Watari was waiting for me.

Again, we sat down at the table and he spread out the map. Without delay we went to the point in words to this effect: "The Minister of War states that the Japanese government will act in accordance with your plan provided the American and British governments will bring great pressure to bear on the Japanese government to force us to withdraw our troops from Shanghai. This, in order that the Japanese Army may save face with the Chinese. This is very important to us." My reply was to this effect, "I understand your position. I will report our conversation to my Ambassador. I appreciate your cooperation in this matter. I must now hurry to a dinner at the home of the Crown Prince. Good-night Colonel."

Hurrying down the broad stairs to the front entrance of the building, to my surprise and pleasure there was Gwynneth in our car waiting for me. Her chauffeur had known of a gate that was open. I jumped in and the chauffeur whisked us over to our dinner just under the wire to our great relief.

At the Prince's we were pleased to find our Ambassador, Mr. and Mrs. Neville, and Captain Johnson, the Naval Attaché. That evening was a very pleasant one—one long to be remembered. Personally, I was in a very happy mood because it seemed to me that I had been remarkably successful in carrying out the orders of the Ambassador. Their home was unpretentious. It reminded me of an English country house. It was located in a beautiful garden in rear of the large modern palace built for the Crown Prince. The party became quite informal. The Prince and Princess handled us much as an English couple would have done. They both spoke English well. He had been educated in England and she in Washington, D.C. I recall how we laughed over their description of how they got most of their exercise by roller skating in the third floor attic. We met them at other affairs and the impression Gwynneth and I formed of them made it impossible to believe that the Prince could be in sympathy with the aggressive Army group that was beginning to take over all the Far East and to assassinate any man of prominence who did not go along with them. Both the Prince and Princess, knowing the wealth and ultimate power of the American and British nations, would realize the improbability of Japan succeeding in the end in her grandiose plans. For a short time after dinner, I conversed with the Crown Prince. I recall telling him how I had often observed evidence of his great popularity among the common people. He made no reply to that statement.

At a favorable opportunity I asked Mr. Neville if I could see him after dinner. He replied, "Yes, at my office at the Embassy." So on our way home from the dinner Gwynneth and I stopped at the Embassy office building. Soon Neville arrived after leaving Mrs. Neville at their home. He and I went up to his office on the second floor. There I recounted my day's experience to him as my immediate superior. His reaction was amazing to me. When I had finished, he said in an angry tone, words to this effect, "Well I thought you had something of importance to tell me. If I had known this was all, I need not have come over to my office at this time of night." My reply was about as follows, "I brought this information to you first as my immediate superior. I thought you would want to take it yourself to the Ambassador. Good-night." Inwardly, I was all upset as I went back down to our car. Neville never explained his discourteous words to me, so my feelings were never so friendly toward him thereafter.

I suppose he did take my report to the Ambassador

because the rumor soon spread through the Embassy officials that the Ambassador had reported the proposal to our government in Washington with the recommendation that Mr. Neville and I be sent to Shanghai to help in carrying through the agreement. Then almost immediately came another line of talk that our Ambassador had received a very sharp note from Mr. Stimson, who told him to cease at once his individual activities and carry out orders only because although he, the Ambassador, might know the situation in the Far East, he did not know the local and international political situation as they knew it in Washington. Someone expressed it that, "Well, Mr. Stimson told the Governor to stand up, put his heels together, pull in his chin, and not to move until further orders."

When I heard that the whole arrangement had been thrown overboard, I wrote a long report to the War Department telling them in detail about the part I had played in it. There was no reply received to that report.

In January 1932, General Araki had become Minister of War. He always seemed to me to be the spiritual head of the Japanese military "bushido." He was much admired by the young aggressive Army group. He stood for a continuance of that Spartan super patriotic life of the Army officer. There were sides to his character that would demand the admiration of anyone. But I have felt that he as much as anyone Japanese was responsible for Japan setting out on that program of conquering the world.

It was in the early part of 1932 when the super patriots assassinated so many of the best men in Japan. For instance, on February 9th the Finance Minister Inouye was shot. In the same month Baron Dan, the Managing Director of the big Mitsui interests, was killed. I had been talk-

225

ing to him the evening before at the Tokyo Club. Just as I was preparing to leave the club he came up to me and said that he would like to speak to me privately. We stepped to one side but at once a young European diplomat came up and took the conversation and we could not shake him. Then the Baron was called elsewhere and we did not have that private talk. He had probably wished to tell me that he was in danger. I have never thought that he and the big business interests of Japan were in sympathy with the aggressive group in the Army. Again in May, Premier Inukai was killed and from time to time others.

During this time, Gwynneth and I attended a dinner with about twelve of the—what shall I call them—the non-aggressive group? The liberals? Anyway, it was the group that was in power before the Army took over. It was the group we knew best. The group that believed in working peaceably with other nations, believed in their own nation keeping its international agreements, was just as the so called super patriots, but thought their country could in the end go further through peaceful commercial methods. The dinner in question was the last one we attended with that group after the Army took over. It was held at the Foreign Minister's residence. There was not much talk. Everyone was serious. No joking. One of them made the remark to the others, "Well, I wonder which of us will be the next one to go." I have always thought that the Japanese diplomatic corps and the leading businessmen were against the methods used by the Army in gaining their aims. The group that brought on the war was composed of certain underground secret societies, and certain Army and Navy determined personnel, filled with ancient samurai bushido, with a dream of Japan ruling the world, and little knowledge of the power that surely finally would be arrayed against her.

About that time I gave a small luncheon at the American Club for a few of the young leaders among the Japanese Army General Staff officers. Toward the close of the meal when their innards were full of good food and wine, they talked to us rather frankly about some of their plans. I remember their calling my attention to the beautiful cars in which the leaders of big business rode about and said "You do not see any of the hard working Army officers riding about in such cars. No, they walk or ride the crowded street cars. Some of that will be changed soon."

Someone may ask, "How did the Army group manage to get back in power? I thought that Japan had been running much like a democratic monarchy, something like England, with perhaps big business calling the turn in the background politically when they felt it was necessary. And I have read that prior to September 1931, the Army had been receiving a very small part of the budget, which had required them to decrease the number of their divisions and made it impossible for their troops to have up-to-date equipment." Yes, all that is true but during this time the leaders in the Army were not idle. Their representatives came to our country and observed our R.O.T.C. in our colleges, our summer military training camps (C.M.T.C.), and our Reserve Officer System. They went back and put into being in their own country a system that was more far reaching than our system. They not only put the military units in the schools and colleges but they also arranged for the military training of all young men in every community, whether they were in school or not.

To begin with their country was divided into areas corresponding to the locations of the permanent active infantry divisions. Each of these divisional areas was subdivided into regimental areas. In case of war, the Reserves to fill up to war strength the various regiments were to come from that regiment's particular area. In each divisional area was an officer of considerable rank in charge of the training of the reservists. Likewise, each regimental area had its chief of training. Under each regimental chief of training were many subordinates, one in each community. This community leader was a reserve officer of the Army. It was his responsibility that all the policies of his superiors were fully carried out and that all young men in his community were thoroughly indoctrinated in the manner prescribed by the higher echelons. For this purpose weekly meetings for drill and lectures were held. Through those young men the Army ideas reached into practically all families. In this way the careful planning Army leaders made sure that the common people, especially the farmers, would back their plan for world expansion. The political leaders and big business were kept in line or at least inactive by the fear of assassination.

In their Active Army the discipline was very severe and the life for both the men and the officers very Spartan-like. After two or three years of that training the soldier went back to his home as a reservist thoroughly imbued with the importance of the part he would ultimately play in the future expansion of his country.

When in Japan as a student officer, I made the acquaintance and friendship of a handsome young Japanese who had just returned from many years receiving his education in America. Some time later, he was called to the colors. The authorities permitted me to visit him at his barracks a few months later. I would not have recognized him. His appearance had completely changed. He had the general appearance of a hard working laborer. He told me that the new conscript as soon as he reports is taken by an officer to the edge of a deep well. There he is

228

asked by the officer, "Tanaka San, if I were now to order you to jump down into this well, what would you do?" Of course, the new conscript answers that he would jump in. Then follows a long lecture based on that situation. Everyday those soldiers were impressed with the absolute necessity of obeying orders, with the honor and privilege of dying for their Emperor, with the thought that to surrender would be a disgrace under any circumstances.

Governor Forbes, while in Japan as our Ambassador, attempted to interest the Japanese in one thing which if it had been successful would have been a very good thing I suspect for our international relations. I refer to the game of polo. The "Governor" was an expert player and a recognized authority on the game. I believe his book on polo is still the best one published on the game. If he could get them interested he expected to import a string of his own well-trained ponies. I felt from the start that the attempt was doomed to failure. And so it was. The Japanese civilians had taken to baseball with enthusiasm but the Army had never permitted it to be played by their officers or soldiers. If they were fortunate enough to find a few minutes of leisure during any day they were expected to get out with their wooden imitation rifles and bamboo imitation swords and practice fencing. No, the idea that their Cavalry officers should have time to amuse themselves at a game of polo was something new and wholly impossible to their minds. The military profession was too serious a matter for any such play. Besides it would be a big additional expense for the Army when every cent was needed for equipment for their expanding forces.

XXI
Extracts from a Diary

Before passing from the period when "Governor" W. Cameron Forbes was Ambassador, I want to quote some from the diary I wrote from time to time, primarily for the benefit of my successors in my position as Military Attaché in Tokyo. All government officials in important positions should be required to do the same. Such a diary could be invaluable to the new incumbent of any important office.

March 8, 1932

Funeral of Baron Takuma Dan

The newspapers stated the ceremony for the funeral of Baron Dan would be at the Aoyana Cemetery beginning at 9:30 A.M. Since the relations between America and Japan are somewhat strained I wore my morning coat and high hat instead of uniform. I arrived at 9:20 A.M. but had the feeling that I was too early. On the left as one entered the grounds was a long table with baskets in which one was expected to deposit his card. Some civilians then conducted me to near the main doors of the Shinto Shrine. There I was left. About 9:30 the doors of the Shrine were opened and a long column of people began to pass in.

Someone motioned to me to get in the column. I did so and then found that I was the only one who still had on his overcoat. Everyone else had either left their overcoats in their automobiles or were carrying them on their arms. However, it was too late to make any changes so I followed the column. We passed the picture of Baron Dan, each bowing in turn and then moving to the right as we passed his relatives, again each bowing, and then passing out of the tent we soon arrived at the exit to the grounds where I turned in my automobile check. After waiting fifteen minutes, my car arrived.

There was an immense display of wreaths, most of which were made of artificial flowers. Present were only two foreigners other than myself, the French Ambassador and one of his secretaries. This was the simplest way of honoring the deceased that I have ever seen in Japan.

Note: The simplicity of the ceremony was probably caused by the fear of displeasing the aggressive group which had had him assassinated. It was an oversight that I did not mention the wreath which I had sent.

March 17, 1932

American-Japan Society

Farewell Dinner to the Ambassador

Some time ago it fell to my lot to be one of the Honorary Secretaries of the American-Japan Society, the other Honorary Secretary being a Japanese by the name of Kurokawa, the manager of a big shipping company. The Executive Secretary who does most of the work is Mr. Taketa.

Last evening there was a dinner in honor of our Ambassador Mr. Forbes, held at the Peers Club. My work in connection with this dinner consisted of the following:

Two weeks ago, I was asked to select the date. This required my finding out from the Ambassador the exact date of his departure for America, and his wishes as to the date for the dinner. A few days before the dinner I was shown a copy of the speech which the President of the Society, Prince Tokugawan, proposed to deliver. The following day they gave me the copy of a proposed speech by the Minister of Foreign Affairs, Mr. Yoshizawa. They asked me to correct the English of those proposed speeches and to make any recommendations I wished as to what should be cut out and what should be added. The speech of Prince Tokugawa I sent to the Ambassador's Secretary, who returned it with the Ambassador's criticisms. They told me not to show the speech of the Foreign Secretary to the Ambassador, but I told his secretary the contents. They consulted me concerning the seating arrangements at the main table, at which were various prominent Japanese ladies and gentlemen and several Americans from the Embassy and the Consular service.

The dinner was called for 7:00 P.M. but I found that the dining room doors did not open until 7:30 P.M. I arrived at 6:30 to find that the Executive Secretary had arranged everything very well, including place cards at the main table and the seating arrangement chart placed on a small table at the entrance to the dining room. In addition to the main table there were smaller tables each seating eight persons lettered from A to K. Each officer and committeeman had a table on which his name card was placed. The committee man could select the personnel he desired at his table but in practice most of the seating arrangement was actually done right at the table where the payment of seven yen each was paid. Mr. Kurokawa saw that the men at the main table received the little cards designating the ladies they were to take in to dinner. If they did not know the ladies we would introduce them. When the doors were opened, we found it necessary to indicate to the rank that they should now take in their part-

232

ners and we followed to show them their places. I then went quickly to my table to seat the group there.

During the dinner the Ambassador proposed a toast to the Emperor, and Viscount Kaneko a toast to the President of the United States while the band played the national airs.

I feel that all language officers who are financially able should belong to the American-Japan Society and attend its meetings. If taken advantage of properly, many valuable contacts for future use can be made. Dress for this affair was white tie.

* * *

April 24, 1932

Military Ceremonies

50th Anniversary
of the
Granting of the Imperial Rescript

This morning from 10:00 A.M. to 11:00 A.M., there took place a formal and impressive ceremony in honor of the 50th Anniversary of the Granting of the Imperial Rescript by the Emperor Meiji.

The troops present consisted of the Guards Division and such of the 1st Division as were within marching distance—all dismounted and massed near the white central covered stand in the park in front of the Imperial Palace. The Army and Navy bands, each about 105 strong, were massed in the center near the stands. In all about 15,000 troops.

The only foreigners present were the Military and Naval Attachés. Although the weather was rainy no cover was prepared for the foreign officers. Cover was provided for the Japanese military, naval, personages of rank.

At 10:00 A.M. the Emperor rode out from the Palace on his beautiful Arabian "Shirayuki" (White Snow) accompanied by his aides and body guards. He was in O.D. uniform like all the soldiers. Dismounting at the central stand he walked up the six steps and stood on the small white platform alone at attention for nearly an hour while speeches were made from smaller nearby white platforms by the Minister of the Navy and the Premier, and the Imperial Rescript was read in its entirety by the Minister of War. Loud speakers secured to the pine trees here and there made it possible for all to hear. During the speeches the Princess stood at attention in line under a separate tent at the left of the Emperor. The Japanese National Anthem was played as the Emperor arrived and again as he returned to the Palace. At the close of the ceremony there was much cheering by the troops by command.

In all, it was a very impressive ceremony well planned to impress not only the assembled soldiers but no doubt all soldiers and people of Japan through the radio system.

Following the ceremony about sixty sea and land planes moved in formation through the rain over the city. The bands, 210 strong, marched to Hibiya Park where they gave a concert.

In the evening the Minister of War spoke over the radio on the subject of the Imperial Rescript.

From the newspapers, it is evident that similar ceremonies were carried out wherever the Army and Navy could be assembled, including Shanghai and Manchuria.

This office has previously reported on the remarkable speech of the Minister of War at Osaka recently. It is quite evident that a real effort is being made to line up the Army personnel behind the aggressive plans of the military group.

234

* * *

April 27, 1932

Yasukuni Shrine Celebration

Today I attended a very formal ceremony for the 531 souls of soldiers who were killed since September 1931, in Manchuria, Shanghai, and Formosa. It was a full-dress affair. Practically all of the high-ranking persons in Japan were there. This is the one big military shrine in Japan. It is located on Kudan Hill.

Upon arrival, I was shown to an inner court where I was seated under a canvas with other Military Attachés and various Japanese Ministers of State and Generals of the Army. On the other side of the walk leading to the shrine were other Ministers of State and high-ranking Naval officers. I counted twenty full generals sitting near me. Assistant Military Attachés were not invited.

After sitting there for twenty minutes we were directed to take position along and near the center walk, all standing.

I suppose that in that inclosure on both sides of that walk there were at least 500 persons of the highest rank in Japan. Outside of the gate we could see that the park was crowded with civilians and enroute to the shrine vast crowds had collected on both sides of the road to see the Emperor, Empress, and Princess pass. I noticed that the crowd was kept far back from the street compared to former days. This was probably caused by the fear of another attempted assassination.

After we had been standing about fifteen minutes the Emperor's car came through the gate and up the walk stopping just at the steps of the shrine. He got out and passed through the first Shrine to an Inner Shrine. The car in turning around caused much displacement of the rank on one side of the walk. Apparently no one had thought of the necessity of the car turning around. Soon the Emperor returned and departed.

About fifteen minutes later the Empress arrived in her Rolls Royce with Dunlop tires made in England, in every way a duplicate of the Emperor's car. Perhaps it was the same one. She and her lady-in-waiting were dressed completely in white. She performed just as the Emperor had done. But her car backed out of the entrance to the inclosure and then in turning around dislocated the military guards on motorcycles and side cars who had accompanied her. Of course, there was much bowing by everyone. The lady-in-waiting, when sitting in the car opposite the Empress, kept her head down with her eyes on the floor, as did also the Military Aide who accompanied the Emperor.

I forgot to mention that prior to the arrival of the Emperor the Princes arrived in close succession and went into the Inner Shrine where they remained. After their Imperial Majesties had departed the Princes returned one by one giving all the opportunity to bow to each one. They were all in uniform and looked very well. Prince Chichibu, the Crown Prince, seemed to be the only one missing. Why, I could not learn.

Following the departure of the Princes, the cabinet members followed by the generals, admirals, and ourselves, moved through the outer shrine into the Inner Shrine, up and down several flights of steps in two single columns, finally appearing before the Inner Shrine where we, two by two, made our bows to the spirits, backed out to the right and left and proceeded down long corridors past a table where two priests presented each of us with one terra-cotta sake cup. While we held the cup in both hands the priest poured it full of sake, which we drank. Leaving the sake cups there we went to another table where we received a package wrapped in a white cotton "Furoshiki" and then moved to the entrance of the park and took our cars for home.

The Military Attachés were the only foreigners present. The British Military Attaché was there in a brilliant red coat with broad white leather shoulder straps and his tight fitting plaid trousers with white helmet. The Polish Military Attaché seated at my right whispered to me, "When I become the Minister of War for Poland I am going to have a uniform like that." I replied, "He looks like the Drum Major of the Army Band." Anyhow, the British do know how to make attractive uniforms and many kinds of them.

* * *

Saturday, May 7, 1932

Garden Party at Prince Fushimi's

Today the Chief of the Navy General Staff gave a garden party at his home near Akasaka Mitsuki for the Navy and the Military and Naval Attachés. It began at 2:00 P.M. and lasted until 4:30 P.M. Guests arrived promptly at two o'clock. It was a bright, sunny day and the garden was very beautiful. The Prince lives in a Japanese house with nothing foreign about it or his garden. Here and there in the garden were little tents under which they served attractive cold dishes and drinks of many kinds, beer, whiskey, sake, sandwiches, salads, cold meats, cakes, etc. There was a large stage in one corner of the garden in front of which were several hundred folding chairs. On this stage for our entertainment were given sleight of hand performances and geisha dances. The Navy band was present to furnish foreign music.

237

At 2:30 P.M. the Prince and Princess appeared. They shook hands with the foreigners present. One of the prettiest parts of this affair was the beautiful kimonos and obis of the Japanese ladies. Apparently all the Naval officers had brought their wives and daughters.

The Naval Language Officers were invited but I was the only American Army Officer present. During this whole year, I have noted that they seldom have invited even the Assistant Military Attachés to anything. It is a rather foolish thing for them to do as there are but three of them in Japan. The Polish Military Attaché generally takes his Assistant even if he is not invited.

My invitation included my wife and daughters so I took along my sixteen-year-old daughter Katharine. She became acquainted with a number of the Navy daughters including Miss Pushimi. They could all speak English and seemed to have a happy time together.

Of course, no one left the party until the Prince and Princess had withdrawn. At that time all stood at attention and saluted. Their departure was the signal for all to say their farewells.

It is interesting to compare the Japanese Navy with their Army socially. The ladies of the Army officers' families never appear socially. It is a waste of effort for an American to invite them to his house. The Army affairs are always stag affairs. The Navy is much broader. More of them speak English and they are more pleasant to deal with. The Army is old fashioned, rather hard boiled, and difficult to handle socially.

*　　*　　*

Tuesday, May 10, 1932

Tea at the American Embassy

Yesterday the Chargé d'Affaires, Mr. Neville gave a reception at the new Ambassadorial residence from 4:00 P.M. to 6:00 P.M. in honor of the Japanese Olympic Riding Team. I had intended doing this myself, but when Mr. Neville suggested that it would be better for him to do it at the Embassy, as my house in Takanawa is rather distant from the center of the city, I acquiesced.

This office prepared the invitations at a cost of Yen 12 ($6.00) per hundred and sent them out. They were in Japanese on a nice card with the Embassy's crest at the top. No reply was requested. I am now inclined to think that a reply should have been asked for. It would have been easy to have placed in the envelope one of the reply cards such as the Japanese use with their invitations; in fact, in dealing with the Army it might be well to send all invitations in Japanese and copy their system. They appear to desire not to mix in foreign society any more than they have to.

To this tea were invited a large number of Japanese officers of the War Department and the General Staff, former Japanese Military Attachés to Washington, those who had recently made a name for themselves in Manchuria, the future Military Attachés to Washington, the Olympic Committee, etc. The tea in my opinion was a decided failure. Almost no one of real interest or standing came; exceptions to this rule were General Kanaya, the recent Chief of Staff, Colonel Furujo of the Press Bureau, and General Osami of the Cavalry School. I heard unofficially that the Chief of Staff also gave a reception for the riding team the same afternoon. Probably this is true as the team came quite late and did not stay long. Anyway, it was very evident that the Army showed great indifference toward this social affair.

In this connection it is of interest to note that my latest effort to do something for the Japanese Army fell very flat. This was to have been a dinner at which the Chargé d'Affaires promised to be present and the ranking guest was to have been the Vice Minister of War, General Kioiso. By telephone we first tried to make sure that the date proposed would be alright for the War Department. We were assured that it was OK. So formal invitations were sent out. One or two acceptances were received but the day before the dinner we were informed by telephone that the Minister of War was giving a dinner on that evening so no one could come. No one expressed any regret to me although I saw several of them soon after. Just why the Japanese Army goes out of its way to be discourteous in such circumstances is hard to see. It is probably a lack of training in that line coupled with much indifference and much feeling against the United States. They may want to assert their independence and show some of that indifference. However, most of them when I meet them are very pleasant. I note that the former Military Attachés to Washington are always most careful to do the proper thing socially. This fact would tend to support my idea that it is partly ignorance on their part of the proper thing to do in foreign social life.

I forgot to mention above that one of the Embassy Secretaries had charge of the refreshments at this party. He served the usual sandwiches, cakes, whiskey, and champagne. Part of the entertainment consisted of showing the guests through the buildings of the Embassy group and giving them a tour over the Embassy grounds.

*   *   *

May 12, 1932

Garden Party at Marquis Mayeda's

Yesterday Colonel Marquis Mayeda held a garden party at his home beyond Shibuya. Among the guests were a large number of Japanese Army officers and all foreign military officers. The American officers came in O.D. uniform as also did the Japanese officers. All other foreigners came in ordinary business suits, why, I do not know.

For the first time I have seen a Japanese military party at which ladies were present. Among them were: the Princess Kaya, Countess Mayeda, the wives of foreign Military Attachés and Language Officers, Mrs. Nishimura, and her two daughters, Mrs. Hagiwara, widow of former Ambassador to London, and a few others I did not know. Again it is interesting to note that the Japanese Army officers did not bring their wives. Possible exceptions to that statement were the Countess Mayeda and Princess Kaya.

The Mayedas have a wonderful home, the largest modern house I have seen in Japan, set in a very large garden. Not far from his foreign-style house is a beautiful Japanese house with here and there little tea houses. The whole affair was expertly handled, no expense being spared. This place is really worth a visit.

With the exception of Marquis Mayeda no one made any effort to see that I enjoyed myself. The Japanese officers stood around like a lot of sticks. In order to converse with one of them the foreign officer must take the initiative. I was rather amused at times as I stood alone to see what would happen and then thought of how the day before the American officers at the tea at the Embassy had tried so hard to entertain the Japanese guests. I think that if one would remain standing still he would be approached by no Japanese, except perhaps the host. Of course, the Marquis got his training when he was the Military Attaché to London. They say he is the most wealthy of the Japanese nobility.

Marchioness Mayeda is very attractive. All Japanese ladies present were in foreign costume, except Mrs. Nishimura. The Nishimura daughters and Miss Nagai, the daughter of the Vice Minister of Foreign Affairs, looked very well in foreign clothes. So seldom is this the case with Japanese women.

*　　*　　*

May 31, 1932

Memorial Day—Yokohama

Yesterday I attended the Memorial Day services at the Ferris Seminary on the bluff in Yokohama. I went in civilian clothes. The American Naval Attaché was present in uniform. There was no one else from Tokyo present. The Americans present consisted of about twenty men and perhaps thirty women, including those on the stage. In addition, there were present the foreign Consuls, the Governor of Kanagawa Prefecture, the Major of Yokohama, and other notables. The American Association of Yokohama and the Daughters of the American Revolution had decorated the stage in red, white, and blue flowers and provided hundreds of large bouquets of flowers of the same color for placing on the graves. A very interesting and appropriate program was provided. The American Consul, Mr. DeVault, delivered an excellent address, except that he said very little concerning the military dead or their deeds which we were there to commemorate.

It is my belief that in the future all Army and Navy officers together with their wives should attend this function and that the officers should go in uniform. I think that if we would do this, the attendance of civilians would be much larger. It is probably the only time when the Yokohama Americans can see this group of officers. I am inclined to think that the effect would be good and that it is our duty to make this effort.

*   *   *

June 2, 1932

Funeral of General Shirakawa

Today I attended in full-dress uniform, with my Assistant, the funeral of General Shirakawa, who was killed by a bomb while on duty commanding the Japanese forces in Shanghai.

About a week ago, I received a card notifying me of the place and hour of the funeral. The following day a telephone call asked if we would be present. The Senior Military Attaché also notified me by letter, stating that he would go, and adding the information that funeral wreaths would be received between ten and twelve o'clock on the day of the funeral at the Shrine. This office had a call from the leading florist in the city stating that all the Military Attachés were sending wreaths worth between Yen 60 and Yen 80. So I ordered one at Yen 80. I had expected the Senior to order one large wreath for all of us as had been done in the past but apparently he thought this was an occasion of sufficient importance for individual wreaths.

The funeral service was held at a Shrine in Aoyama Cemetery. Arriving by car in front of the Shrine we disem-

243

barked. The first thing we did was to deposit our cards on a table nearby. We then proceeded to the Shrine where we were seated with other Military Attachés in about the third row from the front.

Promptly at one o'clock five tall stunning musicians, all in white, came in and seated themselves on the left side of the stage. They had two flutes, a large temple drum, a peculiar old-fashioned instrument something like a lyre, and one more which I did not see well. At some signal the musicians started their wailing and pounding of the drum while the bugle outside sounded what would correspond to the General's march. At the same time, distant guns roared a salute. Following this, six Priests came in. With much ceremony they brought in and placed in front of the casket about twenty different types of food, which were carried on specially constructed fine tables. After this we were all called to attention while the representative of the Emperor came in with an assistant who carried a small branch of a tree. They mounted the platform, the Assistant handed the branch to the representative who then placed it on a little square table in front of the casket. In leaving the platform the representative and his Assistant walked backward until they were on the ground. Of course, there was much bowing both going and returning. After him came Representatives of the Empress, the Empress Dowager, and about twenty Princes. This took about half an hour. We were all tired standing and bowing. I felt particularly sorry for the widow of the General who stood in plain view of everyone all through the ceremony with her family.

After the Princes' Representatives had been disposed of the Prime Minister, the Minister of War, Assistant Chief of Staff, Minister of the Navy, and the Inspector General of the Army each proceeded in turn to a position in front of the casket and read a long speech. The Shirakawa family and relatives were then permitted to go forward one by one and lay branches in front of the casket.

They were followed by the cabinet and various generals and admirals. It then became our turn to do likewise, that is we stepped forward to a table where a priest gave us a branch which we carried forward to another table, bowed, placed the branch on the table, bowed again, and walked away. After about an half hour of waiting, we were able to secure our car and return to the Embassy.

I forgot to mention that the musicians broke forth a second time with a lot of music (so-called) while the bugler on the outside sounded off and three volleys were fired by the troops present.

As a whole, the ceremony was rather impressive. Everything seemed to be arranged to the most minute detail. There was a master of ceremonies, a military officer who managed everything by calling out in a loud voice telling what would happen next. Each of the Representatives of Their Majesties and the Princes were announced in turn in a loud voice from the entrance.

XXII

Beginning *Ten Years in Japan*

In June 1932, Joseph C. Grew arrived in Japan as the new Ambassador from the United States. As far as I know he was the first trained diplomat sent to Japan as Chief of Mission. He had had a long and varied experience in the Foreign Service of his country. He appeared to be everything that an Ambassador should be. With him came his beautiful wife and attractive daughter.

Not long after Mr. Grew arrived I told him that the Army General Staff was running Japan's international affairs; that the Foreign Office could not carry out its promises to other countries or even its own wishes many times because the Army had a way of laying down the law whenever they thought it was necessary. Mr. Grew expressed some doubt as to the correctness of my statement and asked me to prove it. Proof was not then available but I felt sure that I was right about it. It is thought that Mr. Grew also thought my statement correct but wished to have something concrete so he could report it to the State Department in Washington.

So I did a lot of thinking as to how I might be able to prove my statement to Mr. Grew's satisfaction. At last, there evolved a plan. It was based on the well-known love of the Japanese Army officer for a geisha party. I selected the best Japanese tea house within walking distance of the General Staff offices and planned an excellent Japanese dinner with well-known geishas—not expensive but worth the price if we were successful. My guests were my Assistant, our Language Officers, and certain Japanese General Staff and War Department officers who we believed were really running the policy of the government.

Well, the hour for the dinner arrived. All guests were present except two General Staff officers—Majors. I held up the entertainment awaiting them as I felt they would not fail to come to a good geisha party. Sure enough they finally arrived, evidently having hurried over as they were a little out of breath. The senior of the two came to me quickly and apologized for their lateness saying that they just could not get their important work finished sooner. I laughed and said that we would excuse them this time, but continuing in a jocular manner I said that during the World War when in Washington it used to peeve me when some brother officer talked about how late he had to work every day to finish his work. I said that talk never got anywhere with me; that I used to tell those officers that if they would only organize their office properly, they would not be so overworked. The senior Major replied, "But you do not understand. This is work that has been piled on us in addition to our regular work as General Staff officers. They have given us the duty of heading the Foreign Office." And there it was—the proof that I wanted. Now the dinner was a success as far as I was concerned. I could relax and enjoy the evening with the others. It had been easier than expected for I had anticipated it would have to come out later in the evening after a good dinner and much sake. I reported this experience to Mr. Grew the following morning. It appeared to satisfy him.

During this time, I frequently sent off important cables in code to the War Department. This was customary for a Military Attaché and in accord with his instructions. I had long realized that I was the most important contact our Embassy had with the Japanese government because I dealt directly with those who were actually running the Japanese government. Usually my cables contained not only important military information but also some important observations on the political and economical situation. Of course, I always gave Mr. Grew a copy of my cable, but it was evident to me that this situation was not at all pleasing to our Ambassador, and I can't blame him. He was my diplomatic chief. While I was only carrying out orders, I could easily understand his position. So finally we compromised in this way. My office gave him the report we wished to have go to the War Department that same day. On his side he promised to include it in his cable to the State Department of that day after the words, "The Military Attaché reports." Of course, I mailed a copy by way of the Embassy pouch just to make sure that we were given credit for the report and as a check in case of any slip in the Embassy above me.

Shortly after the Grews arrived my family got a mighty fine break, thanks to Mrs. Grew. It seems that when Mr. Grew learned that he was to go to Japan as the next Ambassador, he cabled Mr. Neville, our Counselor, to secure a place for his family on the sea shore for the summer. Mr Neville did arrange with difficulty for the rent of a lovely French-style house in Hayama on the beach about thirty miles south of Tokyo. When the Grews arrived, they went down at once to see the place. Unfortunately, for them but fortunately for us, the day they visited Hayama was the hottest day there had been so far that summer. Mrs. Grew decided she could not live there in that heat. A few days later when I was at the office my desk phone rang. Picking up the receiver there was Mrs.

248

Grew offering my family the use of that Hayama house for the summer, if we could use it. Could we? Just as soon as I realized the grand thing she was doing I accepted with enthusiasm. It was truly wonderful for my family but it gave me a new field in which to work for information. I refer now to the foreigners living in and near Hayama, especially those who commuted every day to Tokyo for their business. The Hayama house was much enjoyed, with the waves breaking on the huge rocks in its immediate front, its broad view of the bay with every night the sun setting right over the tip top of the sacred mountain of Fuji, its fine bathing beach where at night the waves came in tipped with phosphorescence. There we settled for the summer with all our servants, who enjoyed it as much as we did for they had a large Japanese house all to themselves.

One day the family, with the exception of our one-year-old daughter, went fishing out in the bay in a large Japanese boat. Japanese methods were different from ours, but we soon caught on and found ourselves running a race to see who could catch the most large mackerel. Finally, we each had about thirty. It was interesting to watch a Japanese fisherman when we would catch a shiner. He would clean it quickly, and tilting his head back would take the six-inch-long slender fish down his throat in one piece. You see they eat raw fish as we do raw oysters, except that they remove the interior organs and they cannot understand how we can eat an oyster whole.

Upon our return to the beach we gave all the fish to the boatmen except that we carried one bucketful to the house. It was time for lunch so we gave them to the cook and hurried to change our clothes. Being hungry and the fish so fresh I think that I have never tasted anything better.

My experience that day gave me the idea that the Japanese people would be hard to starve unless they were prevented from fishing even in their home waters.

For the purpose of securing information, I visited the foreign-style hotel at Kamakura where I made some acquaintances which later proved to be very useful. Daily, I commuted to Tokyo, thirty miles, which gave me the opportunity to talk to various foreigners doing business with the Japanese. If in two trips I did not get what I wanted from a man, there was no use trying to chat with him again, for by that time the Japanese Intelligence Service would have contacted him and told him that if he hoped to continue doing business with the Japanese government he better not be seen chatting with me. Several times, I had foreigners apologize to me and ask that I not try to converse with them anymore for fear that it would hurt their business. Actually, they wanted to associate with us and give us information but they had to think of their own company which they represented. I could not blame them and always acquiesced in their desire to be left alone. One American sent word to me to stay away but promised some day to send me something really worthwhile and he certainly did. It was a book of carbons containing much desired information about the various industries of Japan. If he is alive today, I want to thank him again.

During the period when Mr. Grew was my diplomatic chief the pressure upon me from the Japanese Army Intelligence group grew stronger and stronger. It was more than evident that my activities did not please them. They wanted to frighten me and cause me to cease my efforts to secure correct information about their troops. If I had given in, I would have been false or at least misleading. I would have ceased to be of much use to my own War Department.

My Japanese Intelligence friends (?) tried to catch me at something concrete—some act which would give them a good reason for asking Washington to recall me. So I had to be more than careful. For instance, several times they had me approached by Koreans who were supposedly trying to sell me military secrets. Now, of course, I would be glad to buy a real worthwhile secret from a worthwhile source. But each of the contacts I sized up as phony. I would have nothing to do with them. But after each effort of one of those agents the Japanese press would come out with scare heads stating that the Japanese Intelligence had caught a man, a traitor, who had been trying to sell secrets to the American Military Attachés. Those articles would always give the impression that I had been very anxious to do business with those agents but that I had been prevented from buying the information by the wonderful efficiency of the Japanese counterspies. This was just a part of their strong newspaper drive to scare me out of my activities. I recall one article which claimed that it took two hundred of their counterspies to keep track of my activities. Quite a compliment, but such articles would naturally tend to make the Japanese people dislike me very much. It made me realize that my life was in danger. Not that the Japanese Army would wish me to be killed. No, I felt that their agents would really be trying to protect me. But I feared that some hot head patriot might elude their protection and put a bullet or dagger in me. I kept in mind that advisability of not being caught alone in some suitable place for such a happening. I slept soundly at night because it was thought that their agents would watch my house at

251

night. Mr. Grew was not without his worries in that same line for the press occasionally took a whirl at him and they said, "Plenty." I recall one morning when I walked in to his office he looked up from his desk and remarked with a smile, "Hello Colonel. Glad to see you. I often wonder which of us will be missing one of these mornings."

Mr. Grew in his *Ten Years in Japan* has given us a detailed account of his honest persistent efforts in Tokyo to carry out his instructions to do all possible to maintain peaceful relations between our government and that of the Japanese. It was a noble effort but the reading of it made me feel like crying at times for I realized so well that he was butting up against a stone wall. While he was dealing all the time with the group who should have been in power they really were terribly limited in what they could do. Back of that group with which he dealt was that all powerful military group which with a word could undo in a minute all the good relations Mr. Grew could build up in months of hard work, and that is just what they did do from time to time.

XXIII
The Japanese People

The writer's knowledge of this subject stems from eight years residence in Japan and over eleven years of intensive study of their language, customs, character, economics, history, and politics.

The celebrated Lafcadio Hearn in his *Japan, an Interpretation,* quoted Percival Lowell as writing, "The Japanese speak backward, read backward, write backward, and this is only the ABC of their contrariety."

I had a friend, Professor Loenholm, who was Professor of Law in the Imperial University in Tokyo. I often visited him at his cottage on the shore at Dzuahi south of Tokyo. He had no end of interesting stories, which he loved to tell me, concerning and illustrating the character of the Japanese people. After showing the Japanese reaction under certain circumstances he would then state what the European and American would have done under the same circumstances, and would always end his story with the statement, "And so we cannot say that we are superior to them or that they are superior to us, but we are just different."

A young American businessman remarked to me, "Say, tell me what the Japanese fellows are really like. We see them occasionally, but I have never been able to really converse with them. They are very quiet and their answers to your questions are always very short and apparently evasive."

I am not surprised at this young man's observations because:

While the American is open and frank in his manner and conversation (sometimes painfully so), the Japanese is just the opposite—reserved, reticent, never revealing the whole of their hearts to you. They are very prone to say the things which they think you wish to hear, and shrink more than we do from the duty of telling you something which you perhaps ought to be told, but which they know would make you unhappy.

Our faces are apt to show our inner feelings, but not so with theirs, for they can smile as they tell you of the death of someone beloved by them. I think they have the feeling that they must not let you feel sorry for them.

We are apt to make friends or at least acquaintances, quickly and easily; but not so with them, even among themselves. I knew two distinguished foreigners, both of whom had spent over twenty years working closely among and for the benefit of the Japanese. Both confessed to me with sadness that they did not know of a single friend they had made among the Japanese. In my own experience I think that I might feel sure of the friendship of one man and two high-class women.

In their character training, loyalty and obedience are much more emphasized by the Japanese than they are with us.

It is interesting to find the importance attached by them to the teaching that there are times when it is a moral duty for one to seek revenge. This idea has more than once been a powerful impellent in their relations toward other countries. We, of course, are taught never to resort to revenge.

The average American still expects to stand by an

agreement or contract, even when it becomes unprofitable or unpleasant for him, at least until it can be changed by common consent of the parties concerned. But with the Japanese there seems to be an idea that a contract or agreement should be binding only so long as it is satisfactory to both sides.

In the Japanese character self-control, cheerfulness, courage, and patriotism are very marked.

Throughout all classes of Japanese there appears to be a greater love of beauty than there is in America.

The Japanese is much more superstitious than we are. He has his lucky and unlucky days for all sorts of things.

We have much trouble in falling asleep under adverse circumstances, such as in the presence of light, noise, etc. The Japanese can sleep anywhere at any time.

In Japan, personal cleanliness is very cheap and is enjoyed by all classes. The Japanese who does not get his daily hot bath is indeed rare. Not only are the Japanese clean as far as their bodies go but as long as they stick to their Japanese clothing, that is very clean, too. But in sanitation from our view point they are still in the dark ages.

Little differences in the way the American individual does things might be interesting, for instance:

In the United States we carry a closed umbrella by its handle.
In Japan they carry them by a flat knob at the top center.

In the United States we either blow out or snip out the flame of a candle.
In Japan they fan out the flame with their hands, a

paper, or a fan. It is considered unlucky to blow
out a candle.

In the United States, upon meeting a friend, we
shake hands.

In Japan they bow low from the hips with their
hands sliding down from their knees, once or
many times.

In the United States, we row a boat while seated,
with two oars, one on each side about the middle.

In Japan the sanpan is propelled by one oar, placed
in the stern of the boat.

In the United States our women, in threading a needle, hold the needle quietly in one hand while
they push the thread through the eye of the needle with the other hand.

In Japan the little seamstress holds the thread mo-
tionless while she moves the eye of the needle
down over the end of the thread.

In the United States we of course sit on chairs.

In Japan they sit on the floor with their legs under
them.

I could go on indefinitely about the Japanese people.
In fact, I wrote a book on the subject just after my last return from Japan in 1933.

Later—1950

How much these people have changed since the

American occupation I do not know from personal observation but I feel that basically they cannot have changed much. I knew that they admired much about our country. They liked our food, our games, and our movies. If their own leaders were to honestly try to democratize them it could be done in time. Without their help I doubt the ability of our forces to accomplish very much that is really lasting.

I am fearful that should we leave them alone to themselves with a Democratic form of government the Communists would get control before long. But to prevent that happening the old families might take control. We must remember that Japan is not long out of feudalism—only about three generations. The Japanese still feel an allegiance to the old clans of their grandfathers.

I suspect that the old patriotic secret societies have gone underground, for the present they are inactive. But sooner or later, they will probably come to life and begin to have an influence on Japan's future. The Japanese are a hardy energetic people—difficult to keep down. They are the Germans of the Far East.

XXIV
Return to America

And now I come to the end of my story, for in March 1933, I received orders relieving me from my duties as Military Attaché and directing me to take the next American transport sailing from Chinwangtao, China. That required us to pack our household goods and beat our way out of Tokyo in just two weeks. It was done but I was nearly a physical wreck by the time I had the family on a Japanese liner at Kobe.

We left one son and one daughter to graduate from the American School that following June after which they followed us on the next transport.

Our Japanese liner took us to Tientsin from where we went by train to Peking to have a short visit with my sister and her husband who was then the Military Attaché to China. It was an interesting experience. We found them living in a grand old home of one of the princes of the time of the Empress Dowager. It was located just outside the wall of the Forbidden City. Personally, I did not have long to enjoy my stay there for soon after our arrival, I ate or drank something that put me in the Rockefeller Hospital for several days.

Well, we caught the transport at Chinwangtao and sailed for the United States via Honolulu, San Francisco, Panama, and New York to take station at Philadelphia.

And so ended an interesting and rather exciting four years in the diplomatic service. It also ended my work in international intelligence.

In this book I have been rather critical in places of our government's intelligence organization. I could have been much more critical. But what is the use of getting worked up about those days of the past. I hope and believe that many of our shortcomings of those days have been corrected or are about to be. In those days we were like a big overgrown child not yet aware of our powers and responsibilities, and too trustful of our world associates. It took time and bitter experience to realize that just because we left others alone, they would not necessarily leave us alone.

Now permit me to say a few words about the quality of my work as the Military Attaché in Japan. I was the first officer on this duty who had both been a student for four years in Japan and had three years of duty in the Military Intelligence Division in Washington handling Far Eastern Intelligence. In other words, I believe that I was the best prepared for that job of any officer up to that time. And if you will pardon the statement, I hope and believe that my work there showed the result of such training. The fact that I was the first Military Attaché in Japan given the responsibility of writing my reports as a finished product ready for immediate filing in the Far Eastern Digest kept in Washington shows that they considered me capable of producing that which they wanted for their study in War Plans and at the War College.

Our government is not prone to use many words in telling officers that they have done a good job—it is expected that we so perform. If the work is not satisfactory there is no hesitancy in telling you. So only through the thoughtfulness of my successor did I receive word as to the quality of my work in Tokyo.

February 23, 1933
Subject: Extract from Major Witsell's Letter
To: Colonel James G. McIlroy, G.S., Tokyo
I take pleasure in furnishing you hereon an extract from a letter dated January 19, 1933, received by me from Major Edward F. Witsell, General Staff, then in charge of Japanese intelligence in the office of the Military Intelligence Division. I quote:

We are very pleased about the arrangements for the Military Attaché's office in Tokyo, for we are confident that it will be in most competent hands with you and Martin at the wheel after Colonel McIlroy and Cranford turn it over. The efficient manner in which the office has functioned in the past, especially since September 1931, has caused favorable comment from many sources including the Chief of Staff and the State Department and has resulted in the enhanced reputation for efficiency for the Far East Section of G-2 which will require all of your and my best efforts to maintain.

(Signed) R.S. Bratton,
Major, Inf., DOL.,
Ass't. Military Attaché

260

Concluding Remarks
by Jane S. McIlroy (author's daughter)

This assignment brought back many memories. The book was first read by me in 1948, then again in 1999, and recently more thoroughly in 2006, in preparation for this publication. I have matured in outlook, appreciation, and understanding since my first reading. Having read both his first and second books, I have been impressed with the quality of this man, my father. His first book, left at the family home in Ohio, was family-oriented. It included his early life as a young man, his years at West Point, his military assignments (including four years as a language student in Japan), his travels, meeting and falling in love with my then-young Scottish Canadian mother while on shipboard headed for Britain, interactions with siblings and parents, etc.

His second book is basically a historical account of events in the Orient pre-WWII, written with his personal interesting flair in covering events. I believe it to be well worth reading for those interested in obtaining a deeper perspective of the total picture.

Finally, I realize how fortunate I have been to have had such a close relationship with this man. Proverbs 20:7 speaks a truth—a truth which reflects my dad's life: "It is a wonderful heritage to have an honest father." He truly lived this belief of "Duty-Honor-Country."

Thanks, Dad.